[英] 埃伦・劳伦斯 著
柯 静 译

万物里的科学

不可思议的植物

植物如何净化空气？

外语教学与研究出版社
FOREIGN LANGUAGE TEACHING AND RESEARCH PRESS
北京 BEIJING

京权图字：01-2022-6892

图书在版编目（CIP）数据

万物里的科学．不可思议的植物．植物如何净化空气？：汉文、英文／（英）埃伦·劳伦斯（Ellen Lawrence）著；柯静译．-- 北京：外语教学与研究出版社，2023.6
ISBN 978-7-5213-4508-7

Ⅰ．①万… Ⅱ．①埃… ②柯… Ⅲ．①科学知识－儿童读物－汉、英②植物－儿童读物－汉、英 Ⅳ．①Z228.1②Q94-49

中国国家版本馆 CIP 数据核字（2023）第 088251 号

图片来源：
Cover, © mycola/Shutterstock, © Garsya/Shutterstock, and © Vetapi/Shutterstock; 2, © Johan Larson/Shutterstock; 2–3, © Valentyn Volkov/Shutterstock; 3T, © Dashu/Shutterstock; 3R, © Lightspring/Shutterstock; 3B, © Dashu/Shutterstock; 4, © Frank Sommariva/imagebroker.net/Superstock and © Zadiraka Evgenii/Shutterstock; 4–5, © Stuart Monk/Shutterstock; 6, © Chungking/Shutterstock; 6–7, © Gary Whitton/Shutterstock; 8, © Sunny Forest/Shutterstock and © Joel Sartore/National Geographic Image Collection/Alamy; 9, © Power and Syred/Science Photo Library; 10T, © Dariush M/Shutterstock; 10B, © ArTDi101/Shutterstock; 11, © Leonello Calvetti/Shutterstock; 12T, © Becky Sheridan/Shutterstock; 12B, © Tetat Uthailert/Shutterstock, © Johan Larson/Shutterstock, © Lightspring/Shutterstock, and © Claudio Divizia/Shutterstock; 13, © Hurst Photo/Shutterstock; 14T, © Jahina Photography/Shutterstock; 14B, © muzsy/Shutterstock; 15, © yui/Shutterstock; 16T, © tmcphotos/Shutterstock; 16BL, © kuleczka/Shutterstock; 16BR, © Julia Zakharova/Shutterstock; 17, © Sergey Lavrentev/Shutterstock; 18, © Stephane Bidouze/Shutterstock; 19, © apiguide/Shutterstock; 19TR, © guentermanaus/Shutterstock; 20, © littleny/Shutterstock; 21, © Diane Cook and Len Jenshel/National Geographic Creative; 22, © Anna Sedneva/Shutterstock, © Pack/Shutterstock, © Winiki/Shutterstock, © DenisNata/Shutterstock, and © Ekaterina Garyuk; 23TL, © Gunnar Pippel/Shutterstock; 23TC, © GQ/Shutterstock; 23TR, © Matej Kastelic/Shutterstock; 23BL, © Vaclav Volrab/Shutterstock; 23BC, © ssuaphotos/Shutterstock; 23BR, © Power and Syred/Science Photo Library.

出 版 人　王　芳
项目策划　刘晓楠　贺舒雅
项目负责　贺舒雅
责任编辑　周少贞
责任校对　夏洁媛
装帧设计　水长流文化
出版发行　外语教学与研究出版社
社　　址　北京市西三环北路 19 号（100089）
网　　址　https://www.fltrp.com
印　　刷　天津善印科技有限公司
开　　本　787×1092　1/16
印　　张　9
版　　次　2023 年 6 月第 1 版
　　　　　2023 年 6 月第 1 次印刷
书　　号　ISBN 978-7-5213-4508-7
定　　价　83.00 元（全 6 册）

如有图书采购需求，图书内容或印刷装订等问题，侵权、盗版书籍等线索，请拨打以下电话或关注官方服务号：
客服电话：400 898 7008
官方服务号：微信搜索并关注公众号“外研社官方服务号”
外研社购书网址：https://fltrp.tmall.com

物料号：345080001

目录

一棵非常有用的树

在繁忙的市中心，一棵小树正在生长。它点亮了城市的街道。它是城市里鸟儿的家。它给人们提供了阴凉地休息。这棵小树在其他重要方面也大有裨益。它帮助净化小汽车、公共汽车和卡车造成的空气污染。

许多麻雀在城市的树上安家。

你认为树是如何净化空气污染的?

A Very Helpful Tree

In the center of a busy city, a little tree is growing.
It helps to brighten up the city street.
It is a home for city birds.
It gives people a shady place to rest.
The little tree is helpful in another important way, too.
It is helping clean up the pollution in the air made by cars, buses, and trucks.

Many sparrows make their homes in city trees.

How do you think a tree might help to clean pollution from the air?

空气是由许多不同的气体混合组成的，空气中各气体的组分是平衡的，包括氧气和二氧化碳。人和动物呼吸时需要氧气。人和动物呼气时把二氧化碳释放到空气中。

Air is naturally made up of a balance of many different gases, including oxygen and carbon dioxide. Oxygen is needed by people and animals for breathing. When people and animals breathe out, they release carbon dioxide into the air.

一种有害的气体

有一种气体能够污染城市的空气，那就是二氧化碳。汽车的发动机燃烧燃料时会产生大量这种有害的无色气体。发电厂在发电时也会向空气中排放大量这种有害气体。幸运的是，小树能够清除空气中的这种气体。它是怎么做到的呢？

汽车排放二氧化碳
cars producing carbon dioxide

A Harmful Gas

One of the gases that pollutes city air is carbon dioxide.
Harmful amounts of this invisible gas are produced when vehicles burn fuel in their engines.
Harmful amounts are also released into the air by power plants as they make electricity.
Fortunately, the little tree is able to remove some of this gas from the air.
How is it able to do this?

空气中过多的二氧化碳是有害的，因为这种气体能把太阳的热量滞留在地球上。这导致了全球变暖，即地球的大气和海洋缓慢而稳定地升温。

Too much carbon dioxide in the air is harmful because the gas helps to trap the sun's heat on Earth. This is causing global warming, which is the slow and steady heating up of Earth's air and oceans.

叶子的净化作用

树用它的叶片清除空气中的二氧化碳。这种气体通过气孔（叶片上的小孔）进入树叶。气孔位于叶子的背面。一旦气体进入气孔，叶子就开始工作了。它们以某种方式利用这种气体使树能够存活下来。

你认为树是如何利用这些气体的？
What do you think the tree does with the gas?

Leaves Do the Cleaning

The tree removes carbon dioxide from the air using its leaves.
The gas enters the tree's leaves through tiny holes called stomata.
The stomata are on the underside of the leaves.
Once the gas is inside them, the leaves get to work.
They start using it in a way that will help the tree survive.

叶子上的气孔非常小，仅用眼睛是无法看到的，只有用显微镜才能看到它们。

在这张图片中，一台功能强大的显微镜放大了叶子的一个气孔。这个气孔的大小是现实中的大约5,000倍。

The stomata on a leaf are so tiny that they cannot be seen with the eyes alone. It's only possible to see them using a microscope.

In this picture, a powerful microscope has zoomed in on a leaf stoma. The stoma is about 5,000 times bigger here than in real life.

制造养料

树利用叶片内的二氧化碳来制造养料！要完成这项工作，树还需要水和来自阳光的能量。树利用根从土壤中吸收水分。水从根部流经树干和树枝，流向叶子。在阳光的帮助下，叶子将二氧化碳和水转化为养料。树利用这种含糖的养料作为能量，帮助自身生长。

树的根从地里吸收雨水。
A tree's roots soak up rainwater from the ground.

树叶吸收阳光。
A tree's leaves soak up sunlight.

Making Food

The tree uses the carbon dioxide inside its leaves to make food!
To do this, the tree also needs water and energy from sunlight.
It takes in water from the soil using its roots.
From the roots, the water moves through the tree's trunk and branches to the leaves.
With the help of sunlight, the leaves turn the carbon dioxide and water into food.
The tree uses this sugary food for energy and to help it grow.

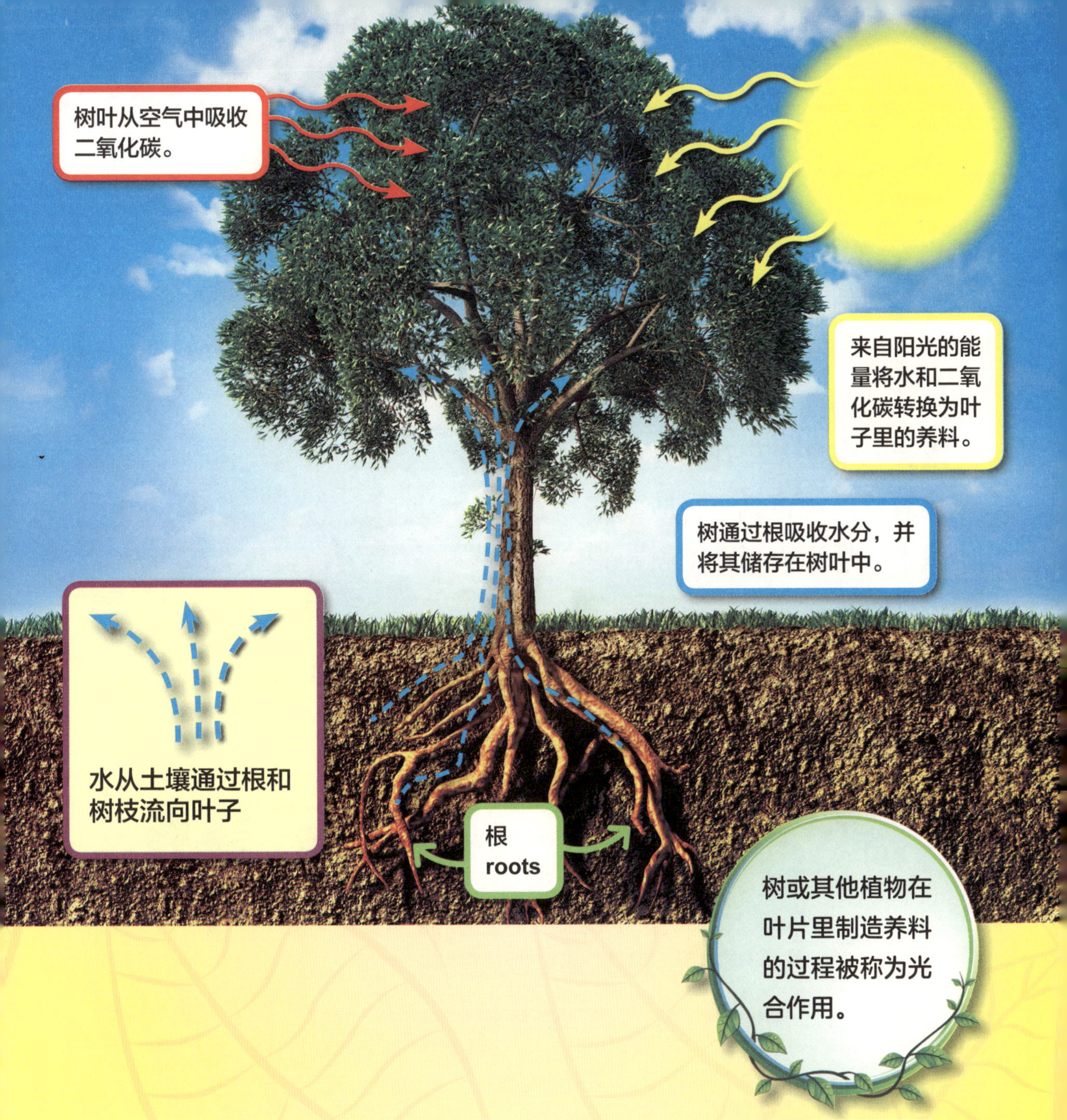

- A tree's leaves take in carbon dioxide from the air.
- Energy from sunlight turns water and carbon dioxide into food inside the leaves.
- A tree takes in water through its roots and stores it in its leaves.
- water moving from the soil through the roots and branches to leaves
- When a tree or other plant makes food in its leaves, the process is called photosynthesis.

制造氧气

树制造养料时，还能清除空气中有害的二氧化碳。此外，树还做了另一件非常重要的事情，它在叶片中制造氧气。树将氧气释放到空气中，然后人和动物就能呼吸这些氧气。

所有动物呼吸都需要氧气。
All animals need oxygen to breathe.

开启一趟寻找叶片之旅，尽可能多地找到不同大小和形状的树叶。这些叶子可能看起来不同，但它们都能净化空气！

Making Oxygen

As the tree makes its food, it removes harmful carbon dioxide from the air.
It also does something else very important.
It makes oxygen inside its leaves.
The tree releases this gas into the air.
People and animals then breathe in this oxygen.

Go on a leaf hunt and try to find as many different sizes and shapes of leaves as you can. The leaves may look different, but they are all able to clean up the air!

树和其他植物通过叶片上的气孔向空气中释放氧气。

Trees and other plants release oxygen into the air through the stomata in their leaves.

每种植物都功不可没

不仅树木能够去除空气中的有害气体，所有的植物，无论大小，都能净化空气。公园里的灌木丛可以，窗台上五彩斑斓的小盆景也可以，甚至足球场上的草也在净化空气，制造氧气。

你能想到哪些可以看到植物的地方？在笔记本上列一个清单。

Every Plant Can Help

It’s not only trees that can remove harmful gas from the air.
All plants, big or small, can do this.
Bushes in a park can do it.
Small, colorful plants in a windowbox can do it, too.
Even the grass on a soccer field is cleaning up the air and making oxygen.

How many places can you think of where you see plants? Make a list in a notebook.

植物对清除空气中的二氧化碳有很大的帮助。人也可以帮助清除二氧化碳，少开车和少用电，这样就会减少进入空气中二氧化碳的总量。

Plants do a lot to remove carbon dioxide from the air. People can help, too, by making fewer car trips and using less electricity. This will cut down on the amount of carbon dioxide that goes into the air.

净化室内空气

植物不一定非要长在室外才能净化空气。住宅、公寓和办公室里的植物也能净化空气。它们的叶片可以去除空气中的二氧化碳，它们制造氧气并将其释放到房间里。

建筑物内的空气可能被油漆和清洁剂中的物质污染。家电，比如电脑，也会排放少量的污染。室内植物的叶子也有助于清除空气中的这些污染。

Cleaning the Air Indoors

Plants don't have to grow outdoors to help clean up air pollution.
Plants that live in houses, apartments, and offices can do this, too.
Their leaves remove carbon dioxide from the air.
Then they make oxygen and release it into the room.

The air inside buildings can become polluted by substances in paint and cleaning products. Machines, such as computers, also give off small amounts of pollution. The leaves of indoor plants help remove this pollution from the air, too.

雨林万岁！

如果空气中存在过多的二氧化碳，这对地球是不利的。因此，地球上生长着大量的植被意义重大。这也是为什么雨林是如此特别之处。数十亿的树木和其他植物生长在这些巨大的森林中。所有的植物都制造氧气，并从空气中清除大量的二氧化碳。

雨林
rain forest

画一张海报，告诉人们为什么保护雨林很重要。原因之一是雨林中的植物可以净化空气，另一个原因是植物能制造氧气。你还能想到哪些原因？
（24页有些想法能帮到你。）

Hooray for Rain Forests!

It's bad for Earth if there is too much carbon dioxide in the air.
So it's important that lots of plants grow on the planet.
That's why rain forests are such special places.
Billions of trees and other plants grow in these huge forests.
All these plants make oxygen and remove huge amounts of carbon dioxide from the air.

Draw a poster that tells people why it's important to protect rain forests. One reason is that rain forest plants clean the air. Another is that the plants make oxygen. What other reasons can you think of?

(Some ideas that will help you are on page 24.)

位于泰国的一片雨林
a rain forest in Thailand

不幸的是，每天都有大片的雨林被破坏。有些人砍伐树木是为了获得木材或修建农场。

曾经生长着雨林的光秃秃的地表
bare ground where rain forest trees once stood

Unfortunately, large areas of rain forest are destroyed every day. Some people cut down the trees for wood or to make space for farms.

人们需要植物

植物有助于保持我们呼吸的空气清洁安全。因此，人们需要保护森林。种植新树，修建公园，在后院栽种植物，都是重要的措施。即使是照料室内绿植也有帮助。虽然我们不能亲眼看到植物在帮助我们，但它们确确实实发挥着作用。每种植物，无论大小，都在忙着净化我们的空气——即使一次只有一片叶子。

在纽约，人们正在栽种一棵小树
a young tree being planted in New York City

People Need Plants

Plants help keep the air clean and safe to breathe.
So people need to protect forests.
Planting new trees, building parks, and growing plants in backyards are important steps, too.
Even taking care of a houseplant can help.
It's not possible to see that plants are helping us, but they are.
Every plant, big or small, is busy cleaning our air—one leaf at a time.

芝加哥市政厅的屋顶花园
a rooftop garden on Chicago's City Hall

城市里，通常没有空间可以在地面种植植物。然而，在高楼的屋顶上种草和其他植物是可以的。这些植物可以净化空气中的污染。

In cities, there is often little space for growing plants on the ground. It's possible, however, to grow grass and other plants on the rooftops of tall buildings. These plants can then help to clean up the pollution in the air.

科学实验室

净化空气

你可以栽种植物来清洁空气。当你的植物制造养料时，它们会帮忙清除二氧化碳，也会制造氧气供你呼吸。如果你种的是生菜，你还可以享用它们的叶子！

Science Lab

Cleaning the Air

You can grow your own plants for cleaning the air.
As your plants make their food, they will help remove carbon dioxide.
They will also make oxygen for you to breathe.
If you grow some lettuce plants, you can even enjoy eating your plants' leaves!

如何种植生菜

请一个成年人帮你从网上或园艺中心购买生菜种子。选一种采摘后能重新长出叶子的生菜。

❶ 种子的包装上有说明，告诉你播种的时间和方法。将生菜种子种在装有盆栽土的花盆中。你也可以把它们种在空的塑料容器里，例如，大的酸奶盒或冰淇淋盒。

如果你使用的是循环使用的容器，请一个成年人帮忙在底部打一些孔。这样就可以让水排出去了。

❷ 将容器放在阳光充足的窗口。在下面放一个盘子来接住多余的水。

❸ 给种子浇水，保持土壤湿润。

❹ 很快幼苗就会长出来。这需要几周的时间，幼苗会长成有大片叶子的生菜，它们可以净化空气。

❺ 记住要经常给你的生菜浇水。

How to grow lettuce plants

Ask a grown-up to help you buy lettuce seeds online or from a garden center. Choose a type of lettuce that regrows its leaves once they have been picked.

❶ Packages of seeds have directions telling you when and how to plant them. Plant your lettuce seeds in potting soil in flowerpots. You can also plant them in empty plastic containers— for example, large yogurt or ice cream cartons. If you are using a recycled container, ask a grown-up to punch some holes in the bottom. This will allow water to drain through.

❷ Place the containers in a sunny window. Put a dish underneath to catch extra water.

❸ Water the seeds to keep the soil moist.

❹ Soon tiny seedlings will appear. It will take several weeks, but the seedlings will grow into plants with big lettuce leaves that will clean the air.

❺ Remember to keep watering your lettuce plants.

附录

科学词汇

二氧化碳
carbon dioxide

气体
gases

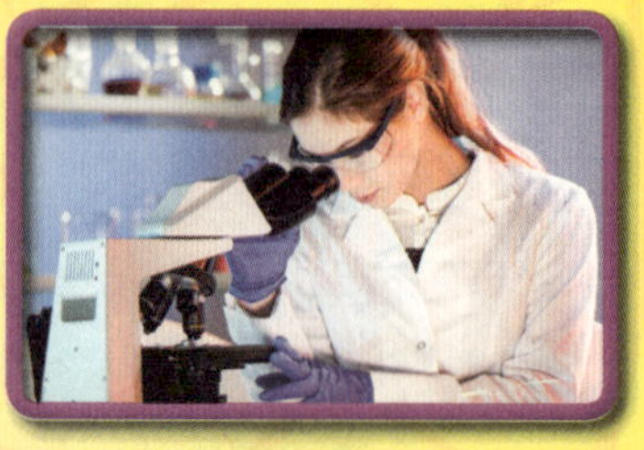

显微镜
microscope

光合作用
photosynthesis

污染
pollution

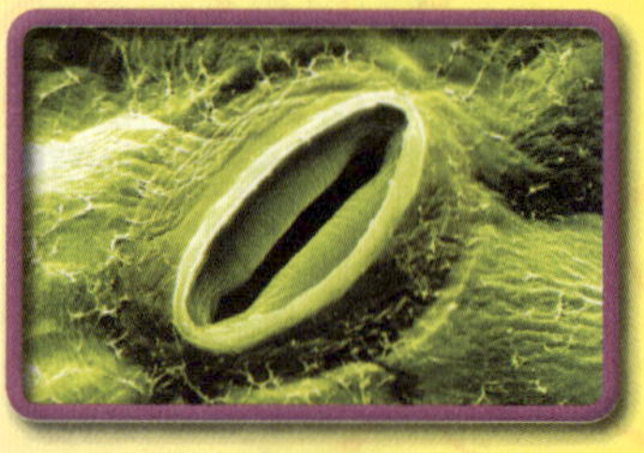

气孔
stomata

答案

第18页：雨林是数百万种不同动物的家园，包括许多鸟类和昆虫。很多人也生活在雨林中。此外，许多雨林植物被用来生产药物。

P18: Rain forests are home to millions of different kinds of animals, including many birds and insects. Many people also live in rain forests. In addition, many rain forest plants are used to make medicines.

植物如何净化空气？

植物装点了我们的世界，让我们生活的环境更加美丽。不仅如此，植物还能净化空气，消除空气中的污染。正是因为有了植物，我们呼吸的空气才更加干净和安全。阅读本书，让我们一起了解一下植物是如何净化空气的吧！

万物里的科学

不可思议的植物

- 植物如何净化空气？
- 植物的传粉
- 种子是如何传播的？
- 用阳光烹饪
- 吃肉的植物
- 天然的药材

责任编辑：周少贞
责任校对：夏洁媛
装帧设计：水长流文化

[英] 埃伦・劳伦斯 著
柯 静 译

万物里的科学

不可思议的植物

植物的传粉

外语教学与研究出版社
FOREIGN LANGUAGE TEACHING AND RESEARCH PRESS

[英] 埃伦•劳伦斯 著
柯 静 译

万物里的科学

不可思议的植物

植物的传粉

外语教学与研究出版社
FOREIGN LANGUAGE TEACHING AND RESEARCH PRESS
北京 BEIJING

京权图字：01-2022-6892

图书在版编目（CIP）数据

万物里的科学. 不可思议的植物. 植物的传粉 ：汉文、英文 /（英）埃伦 · 劳伦斯（Ellen Lawrence）著 ；柯静译. -- 北京 ：外语教学与研究出版社，2023.6
ISBN 978-7-5213-4508-7

Ⅰ. ①万… Ⅱ. ①埃… ②柯… Ⅲ. ①科学知识－儿童读物－汉、英②植物－儿童读物－汉、英 Ⅳ. ①Z228.1②Q94-49

中国国家版本馆 CIP 数据核字 (2023) 第 088252 号

图片来源：
Cover, © JulietPhotography/Shutterstock and © irin-k/Shutterstock; 3TL, © irin-k/Shutterstock; 3BL, © Quang Ho/Shutterstock; 3BR, © motorolka/Shutterstock; 4BL, © Kisialiou Yury/Shutterstock; 4R, © David Maska/Shutterstock; 5L, © irin-k/Shutterstock; 5R, © Tudor Catalin Gheorghe/Shutterstock; 6, © Kellis/Shutterstock; 7, © Corinne Lamontagne; 9, © Brian A. Jackson/Shutterstock and © James H. Robinson/Science Photo Library; 11, © Sue Laakso; 12, © happytan/Shutterstock; 13L, © Scott Prokop/Shutterstock; 13R, © 1stclassphoto/Shutterstock; 14, © kanusommer/Shutterstock; 14–15, © Jeff Schultes/Shutterstock; 16B, © abxyz/Shutterstock; 16–17, © Steve Byland/Shutterstock; 18, © Robin Bush/Getty Images; 19, © Chien Lee/FLPA; 20–21B, © Natalia D/Shutterstock; 21BL, © Scott Prokop/Shutterstock; 21CL, © 1stclassphoto/Shutterstock; 21T, © Kisialiou Yury/Shutterstock; 21CR, © Sue Laakso; 21BR, © Brian A. Jackson/Shutterstock and © James H. Robinson/Science Photo Library; 22C, © VladisChern/Shutterstock; 22B, © Wikipedia Creative Commons; 22R, © Ruby Tuesday Books Ltd; 23TL, © Julietphotography/Shutterstock; 23TC, © S & D & K Maslowski/FLPA; 23TR, © Sue Laakso; 23BL, © Brian A. Jackson/Shutterstock and © James H. Robinson/Science Photo Library; 23BC, © kanusommer/Shutterstock; 23BR, © kukuruxa/Shutterstock.

出 版 人　王　芳
项目策划　刘晓楠　贺舒雅
项目负责　贺舒雅
责任编辑　周少贞
责任校对　夏洁媛
装帧设计　水长流文化
出版发行　外语教学与研究出版社
社　　址　北京市西三环北路 19 号（100089）
网　　址　https://www.fltrp.com
印　　刷　天津善印科技有限公司
开　　本　787×1092　1/16
印　　张　9
版　　次　2023 年 6 月第 1 版
　　　　　2023 年 6 月第 1 次印刷
书　　号　ISBN 978-7-5213-4508-7
定　　价　83.00 元（全 6 册）

如有图书采购需求，图书内容或印刷装订等问题，侵权、盗版书籍等线索，请拨打以下电话或关注官方服务号：
客服电话：400 898 7008
官方服务号：微信搜索并关注公众号“外研社官方服务号”
外研社购书网址：https://fltrp.tmall.com

物料号：345080001

记载人类文明
沟通世界文化
www.fltrp.com

目录

一位重要的访客

一个阳光明媚的夏日清晨，花园里盛开着粉色、黄色和橙色的百合花。夏季是百合花产生种子的季节——但它们需要帮助。很幸运，一位小帮手到了。一只蜜蜂落在了其中一朵百合花上并爬进了花朵里。

lilies growing in a garden
花园里生长的百合花

An Important Visitor

It is a sunny, summer morning.
Pink, yellow, and orange lily flowers are growing in a garden.
Summer is the time of year when lilies make seeds—but they need help.
Luckily, a small helper arrives.
A honeybee lands on one of the lily flowers and crawls inside.

你认为蜜蜂为什么要拜访百合花？

种子是开花植物的一部分，可以长成新的植物。每一朵百合花都会产生数百颗种子。

Why do you think the honeybee is visiting the lily flower?

A seed is the part of a flower that can grow into a new plant. Each flower on a lily plant makes hundreds of seeds.

蜜蜂的甜蜜盛宴

蜜蜂在百合花里畅享着花蜜。花蜜是花朵分泌的一种甜味液体。百合花还会产生一种彩色粉末，叫做花粉。花粉来自花朵上被称作花药的部位。当蜜蜂在花内采集花蜜时，一些花粉会粘在它毛茸茸的身体上。

你认为蜜蜂喝完百合花的花蜜后会做什么？

A Sweet Treat for Honeybee

Inside the lily, the bee drinks nectar.

It is a sweet liquid that flowers make.

Lilies also make a colored dust called pollen.

Pollen comes from a part of the flower called the anthers.

As the bee looks for nectar inside the flower, some pollen sticks to its furry body.

- What do you think the honeybee will do when it has finished drinking nectar from the lily flower?

蜜蜂将它们喝下的一些花蜜带回蜂巢。在那里，它们把花蜜酿成蜂蜜。冬天周围没有花的时候，它们就吃蜂蜜。

Honeybees carry some of the nectar they drink back to their hive. There, they turn the nectar into honey. They eat the honey in winter when there are no flowers around.

东奔西走的花粉

蜜蜂喝完花蜜后，飞到另一朵花上，爬到花朵里面。花粉仍然粘在蜜蜂的身上。随着蜜蜂去寻找更多的花蜜，它身上的一些花粉被蹭掉了。花粉粘在了百合花的一个叫做柱头的部位。虽然这只小蜜蜂并不知道，但它刚刚帮助百合花孕育了种子！

一只蜜蜂在一朵花里可能只停留几秒钟。猜猜看一只蜜蜂一天可能会造访多少花朵。
（答案见第10页。）

Pollen on the Move

When the bee has finished drinking, it flies to a different flower and crawls inside.

Pollen is still stuck to its body.

As the bee looks for more nectar, some pollen brushes off its body.

It sticks to a part of the lily called the stigma.

The little bee doesn't know it, but it has just helped the lily make seeds!

A honeybee may be inside a flower for only a few seconds. Try to guess how many flowers a honeybee might visit in one day.
(Turn to page 10 to find the answer.)

许多花朵通过散发甜美的气味吸引蜜蜂的到访。这种气味对蜜蜂来说是一种信号，表明花内有花蜜。

Many flowers get honeybees to visit them by giving off a sweet smell. The smell is a sign to the bees that there is nectar inside the flowers.

蜜蜂助力花朵

花粉从一朵花的花药传播到另一朵花的柱头，这个过程称为授粉。蜜蜂是伟大的传粉者。当它们停在一朵花上喝花蜜时，花粉会粘在它们的身上。接着，它们为了采集更多花蜜，从一朵花飞到另一朵花，把花粉传播出去。一只蜜蜂一天可能会造访大约2,000朵不同的花朵！

在纸上画一朵百合花。然后给你的画加上这些标签。

• 花药 • 花粉 • 柱头

你可以回顾一下这本书，确保标签放在了正确的位置。

Honeybees Help Flowers

Spreading pollen from the anthers of one flower to the stigma of another is called pollination.

Honeybees are great pollinators.

When they visit a flower to drink nectar, pollen sticks to their bodies.

Then they spread the pollen as they fly from flower to flower to get more nectar.

A honeybee may visit about 2,000 different flowers in one day!

Draw a picture of a lily flower on a piece of paper. Then add these labels to your drawing:

• anther • pollen • stigma

You can look back through this book to make sure you put the labels in the correct places.

蜜蜂把一些花粉带回蜂巢。蜜蜂在蜂巢中将花粉酿成喂养蜜蜂宝宝的食物。

Honeybees carry some pollen back to their hives. There, the bees make it into a food for feeding baby bees.

产生种子

在百合花内，蜜蜂留下的花粉开启了产生种子的旅程。种子长在一个能保护它们的壳里，这个壳叫做种荚。到了秋天，种子已经完全成熟。百合花凋落后，种荚就会裂开。种子落到地上，准备好在春天长成新的百合。

Making Seeds

Inside the lily, some of the pollen left behind by the bee begins the process of making seeds.

The seeds grow inside a case that protects them.

The case is called a seedpod.

By fall, the seeds are fully grown.

The lily flower dies, and the seedpod splits open.

The seeds fall to the ground, ready to grow into new lily plants in the spring.

大多数花需要来自另一朵花的花粉才能产生种子。有些花，如蒲公英和番茄的花，可以用自己的花粉进行授粉。

Most flowers need pollen from another flower to make seeds. Some flowers, such as dandelions and those on tomato plants, can use their own pollen to pollinate themselves.

昆虫授粉

蜜蜂不仅帮助百合花产生种子。它们还为苹果、玫瑰、雏菊和许多其他种类植物的花传粉。然而，蜜蜂并不是唯一能给花传粉的昆虫。蝴蝶、飞蛾、甲虫和许多其他昆虫也从事这项重要的工作。它们从一朵花到另一朵花，吸食花蜜，传播花粉。

Insect Pollinators

Bees do more than just help lilies make seeds.

They also pollinate apple blossoms, roses, daisies, and many other types of flowers.

Bees aren’t the only kind of insect that can pollinate flowers, however.

Butterflies, moths, beetles, and many other insects also do this important job.

They move from flower to flower, drinking nectar and spreading pollen.

为了给一朵百合花授粉，它需要来自另一朵百合花的花粉。玫瑰或雏菊的花粉无法帮百合花产生种子。

In order for a lily to be pollinated, it needs pollen from another lily. Pollen from a rose or daisy won’t help the lily flower make seeds.

蜂鸟授粉

昆虫并不是唯一能给花授粉的动物。小小的红喉北蜂鸟来到花丛中，用它的长舌头舔食着花蜜。进食时，鸟儿在空中旋停，一秒钟内扇动翅膀约50次。花药上的花粉会粘在鸟儿的翅膀上。然后，鸟儿将花粉传播到它到访的其他花朵上。

有些植物不需要动物授粉，它们是由风来授粉的。它们的花粉被风从一朵花吹到另一朵花上。

Hummingbird Pollinators

Insects aren't the only kind of animal that can pollinate flowers.

The tiny ruby-throated hummingbird visits flowers to lap up nectar with its long tongue.

While feeding, the bird hovers in the air by flapping its wings about 50 times in one second.

Pollen from the flower's anthers sticks to the bird's wings.

The bird then spreads the pollen to other flowers it visits.

Some plants don't need animal pollinators. Instead, they are pollinated by the wind. Their pollen is blown from one flower to another.

这张图片中的花是木槿花。试着描述一下木槿花和百合花有哪些相同之处和不同之处。

The flower in this picture is a hibiscus. Try to describe the ways in which a hibiscus and a lily flower are the same and different.

蝙蝠也能授粉！

有些种类的蝙蝠到花中去采食花粉、饮用花蜜。花粉粘在这些小动物的皮毛上，当它们从一朵花飞到另一朵花时就会传播花粉。蝙蝠造访过的植物会长出果实，如芒果、无花果和桃子。蝙蝠给花授粉后，植物的种子就在果实里生长。

在新西兰，有一种壁虎，它们是蜥蜴的一种。它们会爬上新西兰圣诞树喝花蜜，吃树上毛茸茸的红色花朵里的花粉。壁虎的皮肤附着花粉，从一朵花爬到另一朵花。

Bats Can Pollinate, Too!

Some types of bats visit flowers to eat pollen and drink nectar.

These small animals pick up pollen on their fur, and spread it as they fly from flower to flower.

The bats visit plants that produce fruits such as mangoes, figs, and peaches.

After the bats pollinate the flowers, the plants grow their seeds inside fruits.

In New Zealand, a type of lizard called a gecko climbs trees called pohutukawas to drink nectar and eat pollen from the trees' fluffy, red flowers. The gecko carries the pollen from flower to flower on its skin.

蝙蝠在夜间采食花蜜
a bat feeding on nectar at night

团队合作！

蜜蜂或其他传粉者造访花朵时，会发生两件非常重要的事。第一，动物从花朵中获得它们需要的食物。第二，花朵被动物传粉，从而产生种子。蜜蜂和百合花一起，它们组成了一个很棒的团队！

蜜蜂为苹果花授粉。然后，花朵产生种子，这些种子长在人们喜欢吃的苹果里。没有蜜蜂，很多苹果树就不会长出种子和苹果！

It's Teamwork!

When bees or other pollinators visit flowers, two very important things happen.

First, the animals get the food they need from the flowers.

Second, the flowers are pollinated by the animals and can make seeds.

When honeybees and lilies come together, they make a great team!

Bees pollinate apple blossoms. Then the blossoms make seeds, which grow inside the apples that people like to eat. Without bees, most apple trees would produce no seeds and no apples!

授粉进行时

1. 夏天，一株百合开花了。一只蜜蜂飞到百合花上喝花蜜。

2. 百合花花药上的花粉粘在蜜蜂身上。

3. 这只蜜蜂飞到另一朵百合花上。蜜蜂身上的一些花粉粘在百合花的柱头上。

4. 这朵花利用蜜蜂携带的花粉产生种子。秋天，种子落到地上。

5. 这些种子在春天长成新的百合。

Pollination in Action

1. In the summer, a lily plant grows flowers. A bee visits the lily flower to drink its nectar.
2. Pollen from the lily's anthers sticks to the bee.
3. The bee flies to another lily. Some pollen on the bee's body sticks to this flower's stigma.
4. The flower uses pollen carried by the bee to make seeds. The seeds drop to the ground in the fall.
5. The seeds grow into new lily plants in the spring.

科学实验室

种植一些波斯菊吸引蜜蜂和其他传粉者到访，观察动物们的行为。

当花朵完全绽放后，你可以做这些事：
- 在中央黄色区域寻找花粉。
- 把你看到的昆虫造访花朵的情形写成日记。
- 观察花朵中间形成的种子。
- 把种子收集在一个信封里。
- 等到明年春天，播种这些种子，种出更多的波斯菊！

波斯菊
cosmos flower

波斯菊的种子
cosmos flower seeds

Science Lab

Watch bees and other pollinators in action by growing some cosmos flowers for them to visit.

Here are some things to do when your flowers are fully grown:
- Look for pollen in their yellow centers.
- Keep a diary of the insects you see visiting the flowers.
- Watch for seeds forming in the centers of the flowers.
- Collect the seeds in an envelope.
- Next spring, plant the seeds and grow more cosmos flowers!

怎样种植波斯菊

请一个成年人帮你从网上或园艺中心购买种子。

1. 每包种子都有说明，告诉你什么时间播种以及如何种植。你可以把种子种在装满土的旧酸奶盒或花盆里。

2. 将容器放在阳光充足的窗口。

3. 给种子浇水，保持土壤湿润。

4. 幼苗很快就会长出。

5. 当植物长到大约三英寸（7.6厘米）高时，把它们移栽到花园里或较大的花盆里。

6. 如果土壤变干，给植物浇水。到了夏天，花朵就会吸引蜜蜂和其他昆虫来授粉了。

How to grow your cosmos plants

Ask a grown-up to help you buy seeds online or from a garden center.

1. Packages of seeds have directions telling you when and how to plant them. You can plant your seeds in old yogurt cartons or flowerpots filled with potting soil.
2. Place the containers in a sunny window.
3. Water the seeds to keep the soil moist.
4. Soon tiny seedlings will appear.
5. When your plants are about three inches (7.6 cm) tall, plant them in a garden or in a larger flowerpot.
6. If the soil gets dry, water your plants. In summer, your flowers will be ready for bees and other insects to pollinate them.

附录

科学词汇

花药
anthers

蜂巢
hive

花粉
pollen

授粉
pollination

传粉者
pollinators

柱头
stigma

植物的传粉

有些植物是从种子里长出来的。植物在孕育种子前，需要进行传粉。蜜蜂和其他一些动物在植物的传粉中扮演着重要角色。没有它们，植物就不能产生种子繁殖后代。翻阅本书，让我们一起了解植物是如何进行传粉的吧！

万物里的科学

不可思议的植物

- 植物如何净化空气？
- 植物的传粉
- 种子是如何传播的？
- 用阳光烹饪
- 吃肉的植物
- 天然的药材

责任编辑：周少贞
责任校对：夏洁媛
装帧设计：水长流文化

[英] 埃伦·劳伦斯 著
康自立 译

万物里的科学

不可思议的植物

种子是如何传播的？

外语教学与研究出版社
FOREIGN LANGUAGE TEACHING AND RESEARCH PRESS

[英] 埃伦 • 劳伦斯 著
康自立 译

万物里的科学

不可思议的植物

种子是如何传播的？

外语教学与研究出版社
FOREIGN LANGUAGE TEACHING AND RESEARCH PRESS
北京 BEIJING

京权图字：01-2022-6892

Original English language edition published by Bearport Publishing, Minneapolis, MN, USA.

图书在版编目（CIP）数据

万物里的科学. 不可思议的植物. 种子是如何传播的？：汉文、英文 /（英）埃伦·劳伦斯（Ellen Lawrence）著；康自立译. -- 北京：外语教学与研究出版社，2023.6
ISBN 978-7-5213-4508-7

I. ①万… II. ①埃… ②康… III. ①科学知识－儿童读物－汉、英②植物－儿童读物－汉、英 IV. ①Z228.1②Q94-49

中国国家版本馆 CIP 数据核字（2023）第 088254 号

图片来源：
Cover, © Mike Martin/Ozark Nature Gallery; 3L, © Dariusz Majgier/Shutterstock; 3TR, © Shebeko/Shutterstock; 3BR, © Madlen/Shutterstock; 4, © Pam Penick; 5, © Bill Draker/Imagebroker/FLPA; 6BL, © Steve Hurst/USDA; 6BR, © Alex Staroseltsev/Shutterstock; 7, © Rolf Nussbaumer Photography/Alamy and © Inga Nielsen/Shutterstock; 8, © Sofiaworld/Shutterstock; 9TR, © Chris & Tilde Stuart/FLPA; 9MR, © Wikipedia Creative Commons; 9BL, © Chris & Tilde Stuart/FLPA; 9BR, © AfriPics.com/Alamy; 10L, © Shebeko/Shutterstock; 10R, © Lori Labrecque/Shutterstock; 11, © Dudarev Mikhail/Shutterstock; 12R, © Wikipedia Creative Commons; 12L, © Igor Grochev/Shutterstock; 13, © Scott Camazine/Alamy; 14L, © Teze/Shutterstock; 14R, © Mihai Simonia; 15TL, © Anette Linnea Rasmussen/Shutterstock; 15BM, © Dariusz Majgier/Shutterstock; 15BR, © Krasowit/Shutterstock; 16, © Warakorn/Shutterstock; 17L, © Iakov Kalinin/Shutterstock; 17TR, © sunsetman/Shutterstock; 17BR, © OlegD/Shutterstock; 18, © Nigel Cattlin/FLPA; 19, © Avi ben zaken; 20, © Le Do/Shutterstock; 21, ©Sergiy Bykhunenko/iStock Photo; 22TL, © Tungphoto/Shutterstock and © Ivonne Wierink/Shutterstock; 22TR, © SMcAfoos/Shutterstock and © TFoxFoto/Shutterstock; 22BL, © Tischenko Irina/Shutterstock; 22BM, © LianeM/Shutterstock and © Valentyn Volkov/Shutterstock; 22BR, © Jerry Friedman/Wikipedia Creative Commons; 23TL, © Paul Maguire/Shutterstock; 23TR, © Davydova Svetlana/Shutterstock; 23BL, © Krasowit/Shutterstock; 23BR, © Steve Hurst/USDA.

出 版 人　王　芳
项目策划　刘晓楠　贺舒雅
项目负责　贺舒雅
责任编辑　周少贞
责任校对　夏洁媛
装帧设计　水长流文化
出版发行　外语教学与研究出版社
社　　址　北京市西三环北路 19 号（100089）
网　　址　https://www.fltrp.com
印　　刷　天津善印科技有限公司
开　　本　787×1092　1/16
印　　张　9
版　　次　2023 年 6 月第 1 版
　　　　　2023 年 6 月第 1 次印刷
书　　号　ISBN 978-7-5213-4508-7
定　　价　83.00 元（全 6 册）

如有图书采购需求，图书内容或印刷装订等问题，侵权、盗版书籍等线索，请拨打以下电话或关注官方服务号：
客服电话：400 898 7008
官方服务号：微信搜索并关注公众号“外研社官方服务号”
外研社购书网址：https://fltrp.tmall.com

物料号：345080001

目录

水果餐

一只饥饿的红雀正在冬青灌木丛中吃浆果。与此同时，它也吃掉了浆果里的种子。吃完后，红雀飞走去寻找更多的食物。但它并不知道，眼前它有一项重要的工作要做，很快它就会帮助冬青灌木繁殖新的植株!

冬青灌木丛
holly bush

许多植物都会产生种子。种子是树木或其他植物的一部分，可以再长成新的植物。

A Fruity Meal

A hungry cardinal is eating berries from a holly bush.
It is eating the seeds inside the berries, too.
After its meal, the cardinal flies off to look for more food.
The bird doesn't know it, but now it has an important job to do.
Soon it will help the holly bush make new plants!

Many kinds of plants produce seeds. A seed is the part of a tree or other plant that can grow into a new plant.

你认为红雀如何帮助冬青灌木产生新的植株？

How do you think the cardinal will help the holly bush make new plants?

红雀的粪便

当红雀飞过森林的时候，啪嗒，一团红雀的粪便掉到了地上。粪便里面有冬青浆果的种子。种子经过红雀的身体，落在了它们可以生长的地方。红雀帮助冬青灌木把种子传播到了新家！

开花植物的种子长在果实中，这有助于保护种子。一些果实是软的，如浆果或苹果。其他一些果实是坚硬的，如橡子或椰子。

冬青种子的近观图
a close-up picture of holly seeds

苹果种子
apple seed

Cardinal Poop

As the cardinal flies through a forest—splat!
A blob of cardinal poop falls to the ground.
Inside the poop are seeds from the holly berries.
The seeds have passed through the bird's body and landed in a place where they can grow.
The bird has helped the holly bush by spreading its seeds to a new home!

Flowering plants grow their seeds inside fruits, which help protect the seeds. Some fruits, such as berries or apples, are soft. Others, such as acorns or coconuts, are hard.

你觉得为什么植物的种子传播到新的地方很重要？

Why do you think it's important for a plant's seeds to be spread to new places?

幼苗生长需要什么条件？

如果新植株或者幼苗离亲本植株太近了，它们就不能很好的生长。较大的植株会挡住幼苗生长所需要的阳光。土壤中的水分和营养可能也不够养活双方。接下来，小植株还没长大就会死去。植物不能移动，无法将种子播撒到新的地方。幸运的是，有些动物会吃种子，然后将种子排泄到远离亲本植株的地方。

幼苗
seedling

What Do Seedlings Need?

Many new plants, or seedlings, can't grow if they are too close to their parent plant.

The bigger plant may block out the sunlight a seedling needs to live.

Also, there may not be enough water and nutrients in the soil for both plants.

Then the little plant will die.

Plants can't move around and drop their seeds in new places.

Luckily, some animals eat seeds and then poop them out far from the parent plant.

大象摇晃马鲁拉树摘果子
elephant shaking a marula tree to get fruit

大象的粪便
elephant poop

马鲁拉树的种子
marula seeds

马鲁拉树的果实
marula fruit

马鲁拉树的幼苗在干燥的粪便中生长
marula seedlings growing in dry poop

非洲象吃下马鲁拉树的果实和种子。它们走了好几英里，然后树的种子随着粪便一起被排泄到地面。

African elephants eat the fruit and seeds of the marula tree. They may walk many miles and then drop the tree's seeds to the ground in their poop.

动物来播种

动物不只通过粪便传播种子，它们还通过其他方式四处传播种子。例如，松鼠吃橡子，橡子里含有橡树种子。松鼠从橡树下收集橡子，然后将它们埋在新的地方。冬天来临，当食物短缺时，松鼠就会挖出橡子充饥。没有被松鼠挖出的橡子可以在远离橡树妈妈的地方长成新的橡树！

Animals Plant Seeds!

Animals don't just spread seeds in their poop—they move them around in other ways, too.

For example, squirrels eat acorns, which contain the seeds of oak trees.

They collect acorns from under oak trees and then bury them in new places.

In winter, when there is not much food, squirrels dig up and eat the acorns.

Any acorns the squirrels don't dig up may grow into new oak trees, far from their parent tree!

秋天的橡树
oak tree in the fall

一些种类的蚂蚁吃种子。它们收集植物的种子，并将种子储存在地下的窝里。有些种子不需要被吃掉就可以长成新植物。

动物通过排便并把种子埋在新的地方来传播种子。动物还可以通过什么方式来传播种子呢？

Some kinds of ants eat seeds. They collect seeds from plants and store them in their underground nests. Some seeds don't get eaten and grow into new plants.

Animals spread seeds in their poop and by burying them in new places. In what other way might an animal move seeds around?

顺风车

一些种子会粘在动物身上，从而离开它们的父母。牛蒡的种子聚在一起形成毛球。每颗种子的末端都有一个小钩子。当动物经过牛蒡时，牛蒡的毛刺钩在动物的皮毛上，然后种子就搭上顺风车去往新的地方！

当人们穿过田野或森林时，他们的衣服经常会粘上小巧的、带刺的植物部件。这些粘在身上的植物零件就是去往新家路上的种子。

Hitching a Ride

Some seeds move away from their parent plant by getting stuck on an animal's body.
Burdock plant seeds grow together in balls called burrs.
Each seed has a little hook on the end.
When an animal brushes past the burdock, the burrs hook onto the animal's fur or wool.
Then the seeds hitch a ride to a new place!

When people walk through fields or forests, they often get small, spiky pieces of plants stuck to their clothes. These sticky plant pieces are seeds on their way to a new place.

种子不仅仅是通过动物传播的。什么样的天气可以帮助种子到达新的地方？

Seeds aren't just spread by animals. What type of weather could help seeds move to a new place?

随风飘荡

有些种子被风吹到新的地方。种子在空中停留的时间越长，就越有利于风把它带到更远的地方。蒲公英的种子有一个小小的、毛茸茸的降落伞，可以帮助它飘浮在空中。枫树的种子长着翅膀，可以像小型直升机一样在空中旋转，这种旋转运动有助于种子尽可能长时间地停留在空中。

Blowing in the Wind

Some seeds are blown to new places by the wind.

The longer a seed stays up in the air, the further it can be carried by the wind.

A dandelion seed has a tiny fluffy parachute that helps it float in the air.

Maple tree seeds have wings that make them spin in the air like tiny helicopters.

This spinning movement helps the seeds stay up in the air for as long as possible.

枫树种子
maple tree seed
翅膀
wing
蒲公英的种子
dandelion seed

漂到新家

在水边生长的某些植物的种子可能会漂到一个新的地方。椰子树通常生长在近海的海滩上。每颗椰子树的种子都生长在一种叫做椰子的果实里。一些椰子从树上掉下来，漂到海里。它们可能会被冲到离亲本植株数英里远的海滩上。在新的海滩上，椰子会长成新的椰子树。

椰子
coconuts

Floating to a New Home

The seeds of some plants that grow near water may float to a new home.
Coconut palm trees often grow on beaches next to the ocean.
Each palm tree seed grows inside a fruit called a coconut.
Some coconuts fall from their tree and float out to sea.
They may be washed up on beaches miles from their parent plant.
On the new beaches, the coconuts may grow into new palm trees.

在椰子坚硬的外果皮里面，有一个坚硬的、毛茸茸的壳包裹着种子。这个壳有三个洞。小椰子树从其中一个洞里长出来。

Inside the hard outer skin of a coconut there is a tough, hairy shell that surrounds the seed. The shell has three holes. The new palm tree grows out of one of these holes.

喷射传播

有些植物的种子通过高速远距离喷射进行传播！喷瓜和人们吃的西葫芦、黄瓜是同一科的植物。这种植物长着毛茸茸的、绿色的果实。每个果实都装满了种子和汁液，而且越长越大。最后，果实炸开，种子被喷到距离母本很远的地方。

喷瓜
squirting cucumber plant

High-Speed Seeds

Some plants spread their seeds by shooting them a long distance at high speed!
Squirting cucumber plants are in the same plant family as zucchini and cucumbers that people eat.
Hairy, green fruits grow on the plant.
Each fruit fills up with seeds and juice and gets fatter and fatter.
Finally, the fruit explodes, and the seeds are blasted far from the parent plant.

当喷瓜种子从植物中射出时，它们的速度约为60英里/小时(97公里/小时)。这跟汽车在高速公路上疾驰的速度一样快!

When a squirting cucumber's seeds are shot from the plant, they travel at about 60 miles per hour (97 kph). That's as fast as a car speeding along a highway!

东奔西走的种子

植物借助风力和水力传播种子。动物利用自己的皮毛和胃将种子带到新的地方！植物不能四处走动，然而，它们有很多方法将种子传播到新的地方。

有时人们帮助植物在新的地方生长。他们从园艺中心购买种子，将它们播撒在花园和院子里。

Seeds on the Move

Plants spread their seeds with the help of wind and water.

Animals carry seeds to new places on their fur and in their stomachs!

Plants are not able to move around.

However, they have plenty of ways to move their seeds to new places!

Sometimes people help plants grow in new places. They buy seeds from a garden center and plant them or scatter them in their gardens and yards.

将种子种在花园里
seeds being planted in a garden

科学实验室

化身种子侦探

植物借助风力、水力、动物甚至人传播种子。许多种子的传播方式不止一种。看看这些植物和种子的图片。你认为这些种子是怎样到达新的地方的？把你的想法写下来，并与第24页的答案进行比较。

睡莲莲蓬
water lily seedpod

香蒲种子
cattail plant seeds

苹果种子
apple tree seeds

榛树种子
hazel tree seeds

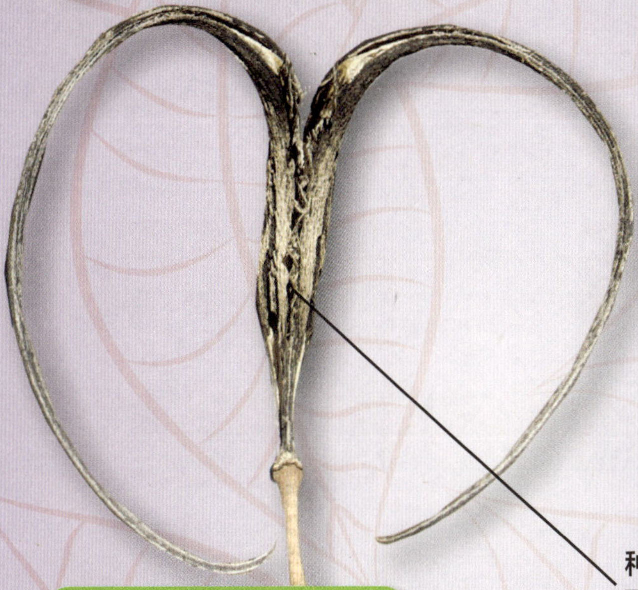

这部分是种子。
This part is the seed.

种子在这个种荚里。
The seeds are in this pod.

魔鬼爪的种子
devil's claw plant seeds

Science Lab

Be a Seed Detective

Plants get help spreading their seeds from the wind, water, animals, and even people.

Many seeds get help in more than one way.

Look at the pictures of plants and seeds.

How do you think these seeds might move to new places?

Write down your ideas and compare them to the answers on page 24.

附录

科学词汇

浆果

berries

营养

nutrients

幼苗

seedling

种子

seeds

答案

第22页：化身种子侦探

苹果树的种子被鸟和其他动物吃掉。

睡莲的种子在水中漂到新的地方。

香蒲有蓬松的种子，可以随风飘散或漂浮在水中。

榛树的种子有时会被松鼠和花栗鼠等小动物收集和掩埋。

魔鬼爪的种荚可以钩住动物和人，搭便车去新的地方。

P22: Be a Seed Detective

Apple tree seeds are eaten by birds and other animals.

Water lily seeds float to new places in water.

Cattail plants have fluffy seeds that blow away in the wind or float in water.

Hazel tree seeds are sometimes collected and buried by small animals such as squirrels and chipmunks.

Devil's claw seedpods hook onto animals and people and get a ride to new places.

种子是如何传播的？

本书介绍了植物种子的传播方式：有的种子被动物吃下随动物的粪便传播，有的种子随风传播，有的种子漂浮在水中来到新家，还有的种子可以钩住人和动物，传播到新的地方。阅读本书，让我们一起了解种子是如何传播的吧！

万物里的科学

不可思议的植物

- 植物如何净化空气？
- 植物的传粉
- • 种子是如何传播的？
- 用阳光烹饪
- 吃肉的植物
- 天然的药材

责任编辑：周少贞
责任校对：夏洁媛
装帧设计：水长流文化

[英] 埃伦·劳伦斯 著
张潆洁 译

万物里的科学

不可思议的植物

用阳光烹饪

外语教学与研究出版社
FOREIGN LANGUAGE TEACHING AND RESEARCH PRESS

[英] 埃伦 • 劳伦斯 著
张潆洁 译

万物里的科学

不可思议的植物

用阳光烹饪

外语教学与研究出版社
FOREIGN LANGUAGE TEACHING AND RESEARCH PRESS
北京 BEIJING

京权图字：01-2022-6892

图书在版编目（CIP）数据

万物里的科学. 不可思议的植物. 用阳光烹饪 ：汉文、英文 /（英）埃伦·劳伦斯（Ellen Lawrence）著 ；张潆洁译. -- 北京 ：外语教学与研究出版社，2023.6
ISBN 978-7-5213-4508-7

Ⅰ. ①万… Ⅱ. ①埃… ②张… Ⅲ. ①科学知识－儿童读物－汉、英②植物－儿童读物－汉、英 Ⅳ. ①Z228.1②Q94-49

中国国家版本馆 CIP 数据核字（2023）第 088256 号

图片来源：
Cover, © formiktopus/Shutterstock; 3BL, © windu/Shutterstock and © L_amica/Shutterstock; 3TR, © Madlen/Shutterstock and © aopsan/Shutterstock; 3BR, © Vaclav Volrab/Shutterstock; 4T, © Susan Montgomery/Shutterstock; 4B, © Jacinta/Shutterstock; 5, © Hannamariah/Shutterstock; 6, © Tatiana Popova/Shutterstock and © Olesia Bilkei/Shutterstock; 7L, © Filipe B. Varela/Shutterstock; 7R, © Filipe B. Varela/Shutterstock and © Mayovskyy Andrew/Shutterstock; 8L, © aopsan/Shutterstock; 8R, © Ruby Tuesday Books Ltd.; 9, © Orla/Shutterstock and © creativeoxfoto/Shutterstock; 10, © Sergey Skleznez/Shutterstock; 11, © Power and Syred/Science Photo Library; 12L, © Sailorr/Shutterstock; 12R, © Uros Medved/Shutterstock; 13, © Triff/Shutterstock and © Vasilius/Shutterstock; 14–15, © Vaclav Volrab/Shutterstock; 16, © Vasca/Shutterstock; 17, © Vovan/Shutterstock; 18T, © Joy Brown/Shutterstock; 18B, © Elena Butinova/Shutterstock; 19, © Martin Valigursky/Shutterstock; 20, © arnlep/Shutterstock and © Eric Isselée/Shutterstock; 21, © Orla/Shutterstock and © creativedoxfoto/Shutterstock and © Erik Lam/Shutterstock and © Ljupco Smokovski/Shutterstock and © maridav/Shutterstock; 22, © Image Source/Superstock; 23TL, © Artur Synenko/Shutterstock; 23TC, © Gunnar Pippel/Shutterstock; 23TR, © Chiyacat/Shutterstock; 23BL, © Orla/Shutterstock; 23BC, © Vaclav Volrab/Shutterstock; 23BR, © Pongphan.R.

出 版 人　王　芳
项目策划　刘晓楠　贺舒雅
项目负责　贺舒雅
责任编辑　周少贞
责任校对　夏洁媛
装帧设计　水长流文化
出版发行　外语教学与研究出版社
社　　址　北京市西三环北路 19 号（100089）
网　　址　https://www.fltrp.com
印　　刷　天津善印科技有限公司
开　　本　787×1092　1/16
印　　张　9
版　　次　2023 年 6 月第 1 版
　　　　　2023 年 6 月第 1 次印刷
书　　号　ISBN 978-7-5213-4508-7
定　　价　83.00 元（全 6 册）

如有图书采购需求，图书内容或印刷装订等问题，侵权、盗版书籍等线索，请拨打以下电话或关注官方服务号：
客服电话：400 898 7008
官方服务号：微信搜索并关注公众号"外研社官方服务号"
外研社购书网址：https://fltrp.tmall.com

物料号：345080001

目录

吃饭时间到！

在一个阳光明媚的下午，公园里的动物们正忙着寻找食物。一只松鼠在草丛中蹦蹦跳跳地吃着种子。毛毛虫从一株植物爬到另一株植物，寻找着美味多汁的叶片。然而，动物并不是唯一的进食者。公园里的植物也在获取食物——它们甚至无需从一个地方移动到另一个地方。

松鼠
squirrel

毛毛虫
caterpillar

It's Feeding Time!

On a sunny afternoon, animals in a park are busy looking for food.

A squirrel scampers in the grass eating seeds.

Caterpillars wriggle from plant to plant looking for juicy leaves to munch on.

The animals aren't the only ones feeding, however.

The park's plants are also getting food—without even moving from place to place.

植物有许多不同的形状和大小。树是非常高大的植物。如茵的草坪由成千上万的小草构成。

你认为植物是如何获取食物的?

Plants come in many different shapes and sizes. A tree is a very big plant. A grassy lawn is made up of thousands of small grass plants.

How do you think plants get food?

根、茎、叶

为了生长和生存，植物利用它们的根、茎和叶为自己制造食物。根是植物生长在土壤中的部分。植物的茎连接着根和叶。当需要制造食物时，根、茎和叶都有自己的任务要完成。

在笔记本上画一张植物的图片。
在图片中加上这些标签：• 根　• 茎　• 叶

Roots, Stems, and Leaves

To grow and live, plants make their own food using their roots, stems, and leaves.

Roots are the part of a plant that grows down into the soil.

The stems of a plant connect the roots to its leaves.

Roots, stems, and leaves all have jobs to do when it's time to make food.

In a notebook draw a picture of a plant. Add these labels to your drawing:
• roots • stem • leaf

许多植物都会开花。花不能帮助植物制造食物，但会帮助它们产生可以长成新植物的种子。

Many plants grow flowers. Flowers don’t help plants make their food. They help them make seeds that can grow into new plants.

根和茎开始工作

为了制造食物，植物需要的物质之一就是水。植物利用根从土壤中吸收水分。水从根向上流入植物的主茎中。然后，通过植物较细的茎流入叶片中。最后，水通过被称为叶脉的细管在叶片中扩散。

水是如何在植物中流动的？在玻璃杯中放入半英寸（1.3厘米）深的水，加入一茶匙（5毫升）的蓝色食用色素。然后取一段带叶片的芹菜茎，从距离底端一英寸（2.5厘米）处切下。将切下的茎放入蓝色的水中。你会看到芹菜随着蓝色的水在茎中向上移动而改变颜色。

The Roots and Stems Get to Work

To make food, one of the things plants need is water.

Plants use their roots to take in water from the soil.

The water travels from the roots up a plant's main stem.

It then moves through the plant's thinner stems to the leaves.

Finally, the water spreads through the leaves inside tiny tubes, called veins.

How does water move through a plant? Put half an inch (1.3 cm) of water into a glass and add a teaspoon (5 ml) of blue food coloring. Then take a celery stalk with leaves and cut an inch (2.5 cm) off the bottom end. Place the cut end of the stalk in the blue water. You will see the celery change color as the blue water moves up the stalk.

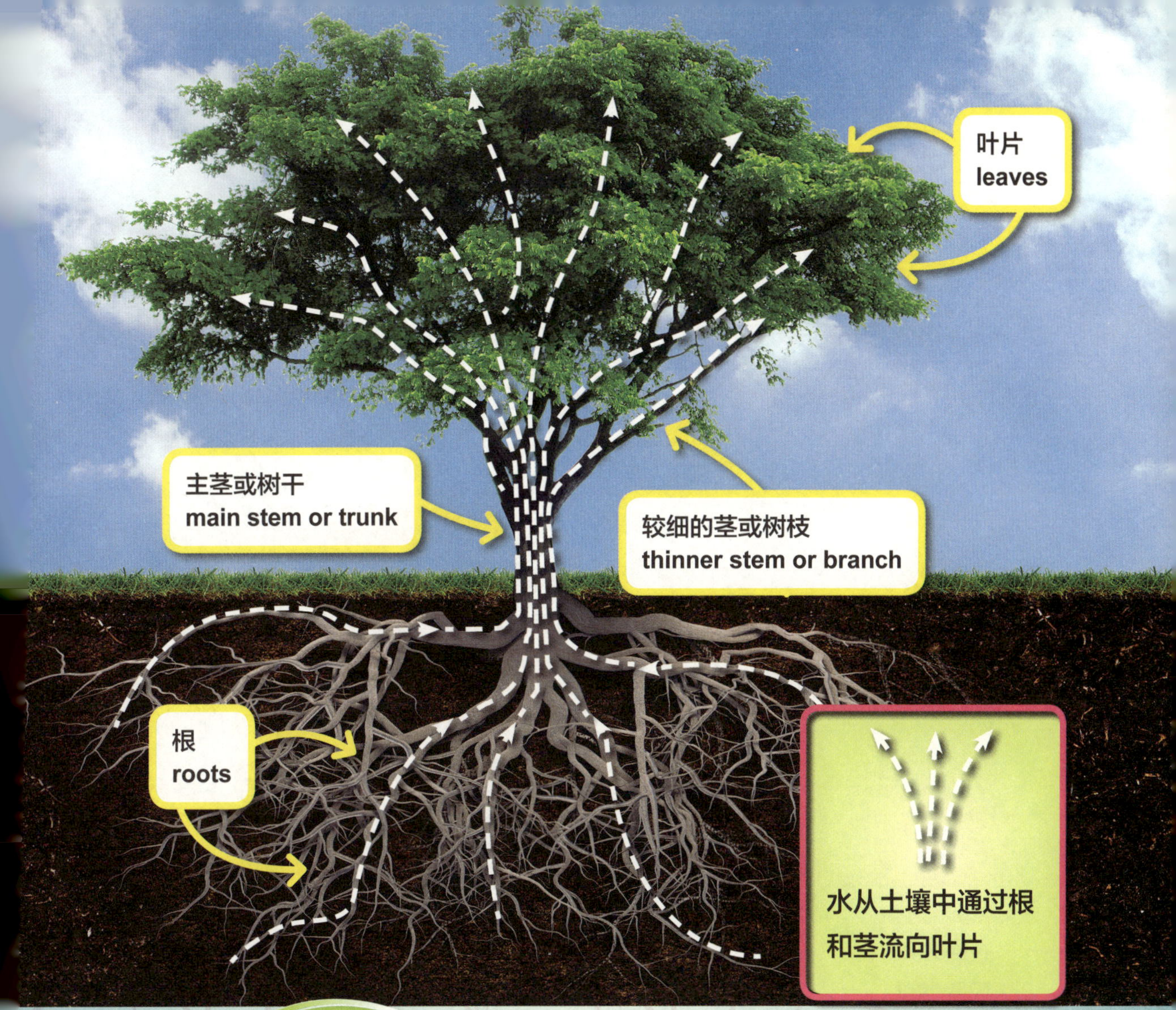

一棵树粗壮的主茎被称为树干。较细的茎，即叶片生长的地方，被称为树枝。

A tree's thick, main stem is called a trunk. The thinner stems, where the leaves grow, are called branches.

water moving from the soil through the roots and stems to the leaves

叶片开始工作

植物还需要空气中含有的一种气体来制造它们的食物。它们用自己的叶片收集这种名为二氧化碳的气体。二氧化碳通过小孔进入植物的叶片。

The Leaves Get to Work

Plants also need a gas from the air to make their food.

They collect this gas, called carbon dioxide, using their leaves.

Carbon dioxide enters a plant's leaves through tiny holes.

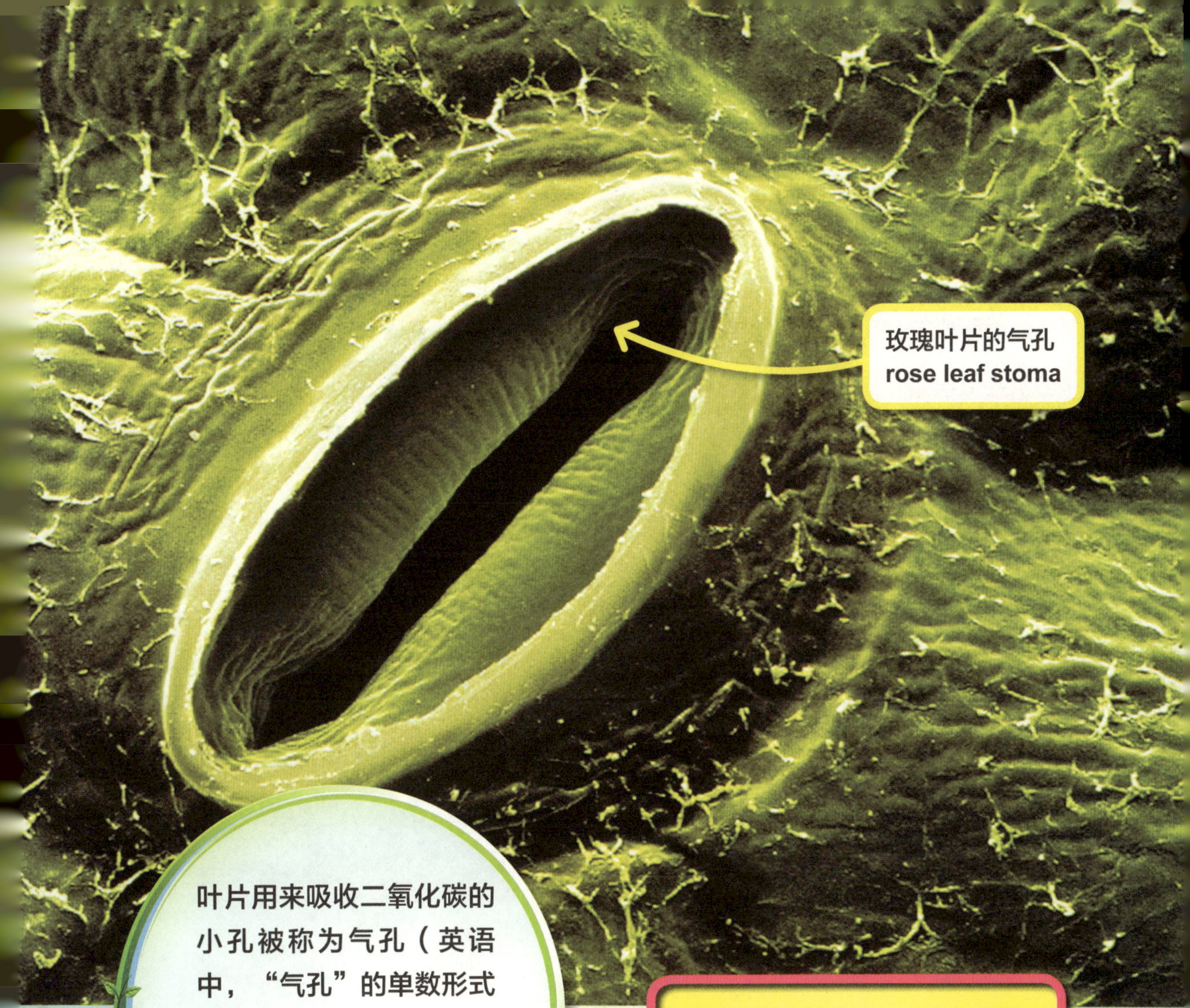

叶片用来吸收二氧化碳的小孔被称为气孔（英语中，“气孔”的单数形式是“stoma”，复数形式是“stomata”）。气孔位于叶片背面。

气孔是如此之小，只有在显微镜下才能看到。在这张照片中，显微镜放大了一个玫瑰叶上的气孔。这个气孔是实际大小的5,000倍!

- The tiny holes that leaves use to take in carbon dioxide are called stomata. A single hole is called a stoma. The stomata are on the underside of a leaf.
- Stomata are so tiny they can only be seen under a microscope. In this photograph, a microscope has zoomed in on a rose leaf stoma. The stoma is 5,000 times bigger than in real life!

吸收阳光

植物制造食物所需的最后一样东西是阳光。植物用它的叶片吸收阳光。当拥有了水、二氧化碳和阳光，植物就有了制造食物所需的一切原料！

Soaking Up Sunshine

The final thing that plants need to make their food is sunlight.

A plant soaks up sunlight using its leaves.

When a plant has water, carbon dioxide, and sunlight, it has everything it needs to get cooking!

叶片可大可小，可长可圆，有的有光泽，有的甚至是带刺的。无论它们外观如何，所有的叶片都能储存水分，收集二氧化碳，并吸收阳光。

开始一次寻找叶片之旅吧，寻找尽量多的不同大小和形状的树叶。找出叶脉，你可能需要用放大镜才能看到其中一些叶脉。

- Leaves can be big, small, long, round, shiny, and even prickly. No matter how they look, all leaves hold water, collect carbon dioxide, and soak up sunlight.
- Go on a leaf hunt and try to find as many different sizes and shapes of leaves as you can. Look for the veins. You might need to use a magnifying glass to see some of them.

用阳光烹饪

在叶片中，植物利用阳光将水和二氧化碳变成含糖的食物，这个过程被称为光合作用。

植物制造的食物与人们用来制作蛋糕和其他甜食的糖并不一样，它是一种植物用来储存能量并帮助自身生长的含糖有机物。

英文中“photo”这个词的意思是“光”，“合成”一词的意思是“放在一起”。因此，光合作用的意思是“用光来合成”。

Cooking with Sunshine

Inside their leaves, plants use sunlight to turn water and carbon dioxide into a sugary food.

This process is called photosynthesis.

The food a plant makes is not the same as the sugar that people use to make cakes and other sweet foods.

It's a kind of sugar that plants use for energy and to help them grow.

The word "photo" means "light." The word "synthesis" means "putting together." So photosynthesis means "putting together with light."

绿色烹饪

光合作用是在植物的叶片中进行的，需借助一种叫做叶绿素的物质。叶绿素使植物呈现绿色。它还能捕获阳光中的能量。叶绿素利用这些能量在植物的叶片中进行光合作用。

Cooking Green

Photosynthesis takes place in a plant's leaves with the help of a substance called chlorophyll.

Chlorophyll gives plants their green color.

It also traps the energy in sunlight.

Chlorophyll uses that energy to make photosynthesis happen in the plant's leaves.

阳光除了帮助植物制造食物外，还帮助植物在叶片中制造叶绿素。

In addition to helping a plant make food, sunlight helps a plant make chlorophyll in its leaves.

神奇的植物

在光合作用过程中，植物不仅制造食物，其他令人惊叹的事情也在发生！植物还能制造一种叫做氧气的气体。植物的叶片释放出氧气。人和动物的呼吸需要这种气体。没有植物提供的氧气，人和动物就会死亡。

Amazing Plants

During photosynthesis, plants don't just make their food.

Something else amazing happens!

Plants make a gas called oxygen.

They give off the oxygen from their leaves.

People and animals need this gas to breathe.

Without oxygen from plants, people and animals would die.

植物不仅会制造氧气来帮助人们，它们还为人们提供食物。在过去的一周里，你吃过哪些植物？

（第24页有一些想法可以帮助你。）

People can't see it happening but all around them plants are making oxygen—from little houseplants on windowsills to grass and tall trees in backyards.

Plants don't only help people by making oxygen. Plants also give people food. What plants have you eaten in the past week?

(There are some ideas to help you on page 24.)

人类和动物都需要植物！

植物利用水、二氧化碳和阳光来制造食物，从而生长和生存。当植物制造食物时，会释放氧气。人类和动物都需要氧气来呼吸。如果没有人类和动物，许多植物仍然可以在地球上存活。但如果没有植物，人类和动物就没有了赖以生存的氧气。

植物从它们制造的食物中获取能量。为了保持健康，它们还需要从土壤中获取营养。它们通过根摄取营养物质。

People and Animals Need Plants!

Plants grow and live by making food from water, carbon dioxide, and sunlight.

As they make food, they give off oxygen.

Humans and animals need oxygen to breathe.

Many plants could survive on Earth without people and animals.

Without plants, however, people and animals wouldn't have the oxygen they need to live.

Plants get energy from the food they make. To stay healthy, they also need nutrients from the soil. They take in nutrients through their roots.

光合作用在进行

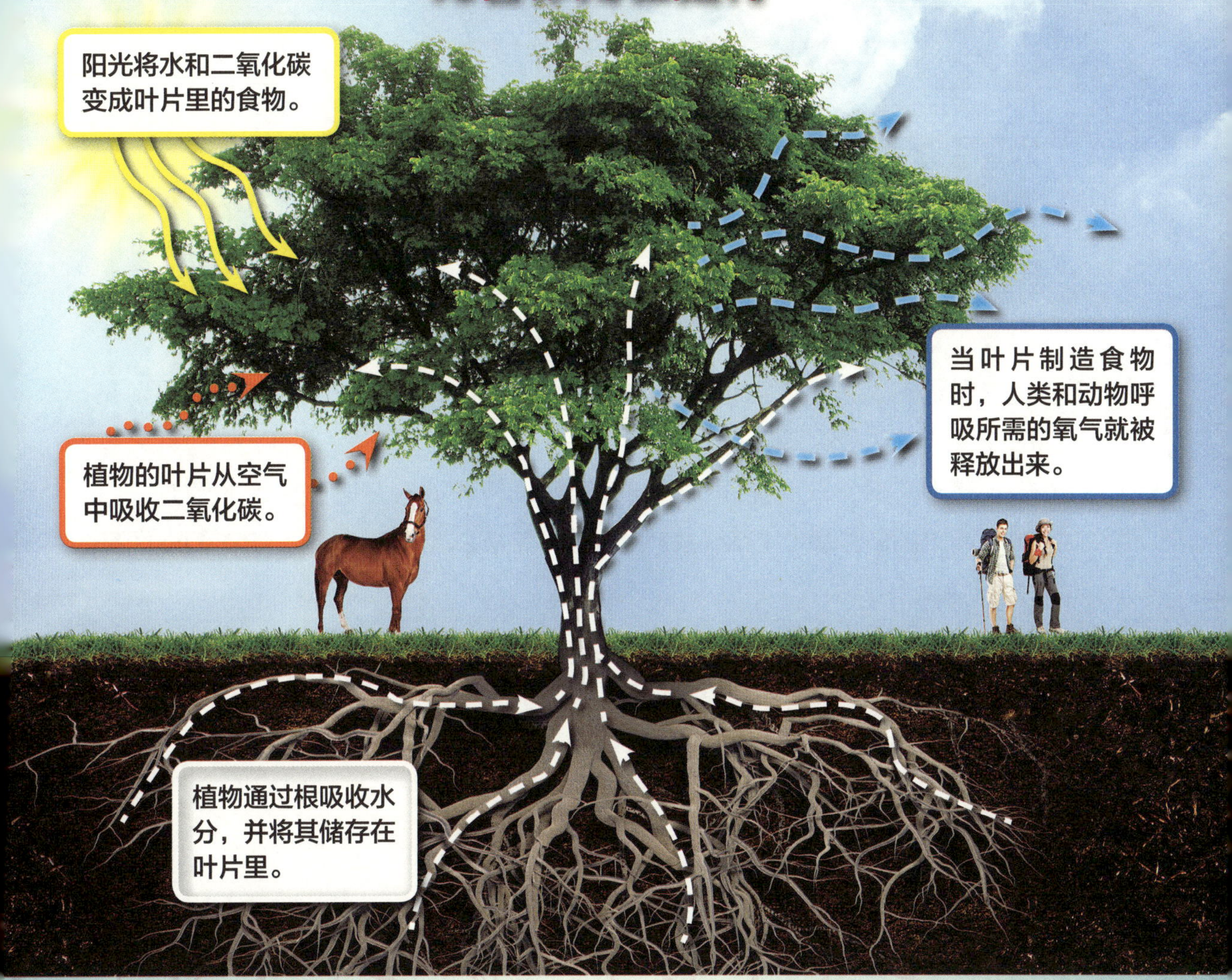

Photosynthesis in Action

- Sunlight turns water and carbon dioxide into food inside the leaves.
- A plant's leaves take in carbon dioxide from the air.
- A plant takes in water through its roots and stores it in its leaves.
- As the leaves make food, oxygen that people and animals need to breathe is given off.

科学实验室

阳光实验

植物需要阳光来制造食物以及叶片中绿色的叶绿素。如果植物没有得到充分的阳光，会发生什么呢?

为了找出答案，取两盆同样的绿叶植物。将一株放在阳光充足的地方，另一株放在黑暗的壁橱里。给两株植物浇水，保持其土壤湿润。（给它们浇同样多的水。）

每隔三四天比较一下你的植物。你发现了什么?

（可以在第24页找到这个实验的答案。）

Science Lab

Sunlight Experiment

A plant needs sunlight to make both its food and the green chlorophyll in its leaves.

What happens when a plant doesn't get enough sunlight?

To find out, take two potted plants of the same kind that have green leaves.

Place one plant in a sunny place and the other in a dark closet.

Water the plants to keep their soil moist. (Give them both the same amount of water.)

Compare your plants every three or four days.

What do you notice happening?

(You can find out what will happen in this experiment on page 24.)

附录

科学词汇

叶绿素
chlorophyll

能量
energy

气体
gas

营养
nutrients

光合作用
photosynthesis

根
roots

答案

第19页：所有水果和蔬菜都来自植物。面包、饼干和麦片都是由玉米和小麦等植物制成。这些植物属于禾本科植物，称为谷物。

第22页：壁橱里的植物看起来没有另一株植物健康。因为没有阳光，它不能制造食物。除此之外，它的叶片可能开始发白，因为它需要阳光来制造绿色的叶绿素。不过，要有耐心！可能要过几个星期才能看到这些变化。

P19: All fruits and vegetables come from plants. Bread, cookies, and cereal are made from plants such as corn and wheat. These plants are types of grass, called grains.

P22: The plant in the closet will not look as healthy as the other plant. That's because it cannot make food without sunlight. Also, its leaves may start to look pale because it needs sunlight to make green chlorophyll. Be patient, though! It may be several weeks before you see these changes happen.

用阳光烹饪

本书介绍了植物如何进行光合作用。与动物不同，植物不能四处行走寻找食物，它们要靠自己制造食物。植物利用阳光合成食物，在光合作用的过程中，它们还能吸收二氧化碳，制造氧气。让我们一起来了解一下植物是如何用阳光进行烹饪的吧！

万物里的科学

不可思议的植物

植物如何净化空气？
植物的传粉
种子是如何传播的？
• 用阳光烹饪
吃肉的植物
天然的药材

责任编辑：周少贞
责任校对：夏洁媛
装帧设计：水长流文化

[英] 埃伦 • 劳伦斯 著
柯 静 译

万物里的科学

不可思议的植物

吃肉的植物

外语教学与研究出版社
FOREIGN LANGUAGE TEACHING AND RESEARCH PRESS

[英] 埃伦•劳伦斯 著
柯　静译

万物里的科学

不可思议的植物

吃肉的植物

外语教学与研究出版社
FOREIGN LANGUAGE TEACHING AND RESEARCH PRESS
北京　BEIJING

京权图字：01-2022-6892

图书在版编目（CIP）数据

万物里的科学．不可思议的植物．吃肉的植物 ：汉文、英文 /（英）埃伦 · 劳伦斯（Ellen Lawrence）著 ；柯静译．-- 北京 ：外语教学与研究出版社，2023.6
ISBN 978-7-5213-4508-7

Ⅰ．①万… Ⅱ．①埃… ②柯… Ⅲ．①科学知识－儿童读物－汉、英②植物－儿童读物－汉、英 Ⅳ．①Z228.1②Q94-49

中国国家版本馆 CIP 数据核字（2023）第 088255 号

地图审图号：GS 京（2023）0971 号

图片来源：
Cover, © Cathy Keifer/Shutterstock and © Daniel Gale/Shutterstock; 3, © Lazar Mihai-Bogdan/Shutterstock; 4, © Marvin Dembinsky/Photo Associates/Alamy; 5, © a9photo/Shutterstock and © Cathy Keifer/Shutterstock; 6, © Alessandro Zocc/Shutterstock; 7, © Chris Mattison/FLPA; 8B, © Cosmographics; 8–9, © Juniors/Superstock; 10, © Lazar Mihai-Bogdan/Shutterstock; 11, © Jaime Pharr/Shutterstock; 12, © Jan Van Arkel/FN/Minden/FLPA; 13, © Minden Pictures/Superstock; 13TR, © Cosmographics; 14T, © Peter Bulsing/FN/Minden/FLPA; 14B, © Cosmographics; 15, © Claude Nuridsany & Marie Perennou/Science Photo Library; 15TR, © blickwinkel/Alamy; 16B, © Cosmographics; 16R, © Photo Researchers/FLPA; 17, © Nature's Images/Science Photo Library; 18T, © Inga Spence/FLPA; 18B, © Cosmographics; 19L, © Noah Elhardt/Wikipedia Creative Commons; 19R, © EcoPrint/Shutterstock; 20–21, © Mike Stutz/Bearcats Photography; 21R, © Ch'ien Lee/Wikipedia Creative Commons; 22L, © Ruby Tuesday Books Ltd; 22TM, © Galushko Sergey/Shutterstock and © aquariagirl1970/Shutterstock; 22TR, © Ruby Tuesday Books Ltd; 22BM, © Danny Smythe/Shutterstock; 22BR, © picturepartners/Shutterstock; 23TL, © Jaime Pharr/Shutterstock; 23TC, © Lazar Mihai-Bogdan/Shutterstock; 23TR, © a9photo/Shutterstock and © Cathy Keifer/Shutterstock; 23BL, © Mike Stutz/Bearcats Photography; 23BC, © Minden Pictures/Superstock; 23BR, © Lazar Mihai-Bogdan/Shutterstock.

出 版 人　王　芳
项目策划　刘晓楠　贺舒雅
项目负责　贺舒雅
责任编辑　周少贞
责任校对　夏洁媛
装帧设计　水长流文化
出版发行　外语教学与研究出版社
社　　址　北京市西三环北路 19 号（100089）
网　　址　https://www.fltrp.com
印　　刷　天津善印科技有限公司
开　　本　787×1092　1/16
印　　张　9
版　　次　2023 年 6 月第 1 版
　　　　　2023 年 6 月第 1 次印刷
书　　号　ISBN 978-7-5213-4508-7
定　　价　83.00 元（全 6 册）

如有图书采购需求，图书内容或印刷装订等问题，侵权、盗版书籍等线索，请拨打以下电话或关注官方服务号：
客服电话：400 898 7008
官方服务号：微信搜索并关注公众号“外研社官方服务号”
外研社购书网址：https://fltrp.tmall.com

物料号：345080001

记载人类文明
沟通世界文化
www.fltrp.com

目录

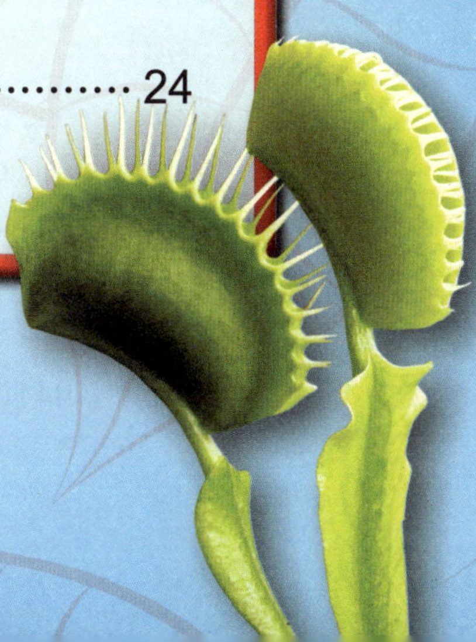

身陷囹圄！

一只苍蝇绕着一株小巧的植物嗡嗡地飞，落在了它红色的叶子上。这只昆虫还不知道，但它刚才犯了个大错。它停在了一株名为维纳斯捕蝇草的植物上。突然，叶片合上了！苍蝇成了这株植物的俘虏，无处可逃。

维纳斯捕蝇草的叶子
Venus flytrap leaf

你觉得这株植物为什么要捉住这只苍蝇呢?

Trapped!

A fly buzzing around a small plant lands on one of its red leaves.
The insect doesn't know it, but it has just made a big mistake.
It has landed on a plant called a Venus flytrap.
Suddenly, the leaf snaps shut!
The fly is now the plant's prisoner, and there is no escape.

Why do you think the plant has trapped the fly?

有些维纳斯捕蝇草的叶子内有刚毛。这些叶子是捕虫陷阱，如果有东西碰到了它们的刚毛，比如一只昆虫，叶子就会突然合上。

Some of the leaves on a Venus flytrap have little hairs. These leaves act as a trap by snapping shut when something, such as an insect, touches the hairs.

食肉植物

维纳斯捕蝇草捕捉苍蝇以获取维持健康所需的营养。大部分植物都不是通过这种方式获取营养的，它们通过根从土壤中吸收营养。然而，有些植物生长的土壤里几乎没有营养。这些植物，比如维纳斯捕蝇草，以昆虫和蜘蛛为食，获取营养，它们被称作食肉植物。

你认为维纳斯捕蝇草是如何从动物的身体中获得它所需要的营养的？

Meat-Eating Plants

The Venus flytrap caught the fly to get the nutrients it needs to stay healthy.
Most plants don't get nutrients this way.
They take them in from the soil through their roots.
Some plants, however, grow in places where there are few nutrients in the soil.
These plants, such as the Venus flytrap, eat insects and spiders to get nutrients.
They are known as meat-eating plants.

How do you think a Venus flytrap gets the nutrients it needs from an animal's body?

氮是食肉植物从昆虫身上获取的营养元素之一。植物的生长需要氮，特别是它们的叶子需要氮元素。

One of the nutrients that meat-eating plants get from feeding on insects is nitrogen. Plants need nitrogen to help them grow—especially their leaves.

别了，苍蝇！

一旦维纳斯捕蝇草抓到了苍蝇，叶子就马上闭合。然后叶片分泌出消化液，分解苍蝇身体柔软的部分。这种汁液的工作原理就像人的胃消化食物一样。苍蝇逐渐变得又软又黏，叶片吸干昆虫身体里的营养物质。大约五天后，叶片重新打开，苍蝇只剩下干枯的躯壳！

捕蝇草生长在红色标示区域。它们长在湿软的沼泽里。

Good-bye, Fly!

Once a Venus flytrap catches a fly, the leafy trap squeezes shut.
Then the trap oozes juices that break down the soft parts of the fly's body.
The juices work like the liquids that break down food in a person's stomach.
As the fly becomes soft and soupy, the trap soaks up nutrients from the insect's body.
After about five days, the trap opens back up, and all that is left of the fly is its dry shell!

Venus flytraps live in the area shown in red. They grow in places called bogs where the ground is wet and soft.

身陷囹圄的苍蝇
fly inside trap

维纳斯捕蝇草的叶片，或者说捕虫陷阱，分泌一种有甜味的液体，叫做糖浆。苍蝇和其他昆虫为了吸食糖浆被引诱到陷阱里。

The leaves, or traps, of a Venus flytrap make a sweet liquid called nectar. Flies and other insects are attracted to the traps to eat the nectar.

制造养料，储存能量

为了生存和生长，食肉植物不仅需要从昆虫中吸收养分，它们还需要制造养料，储存能量。它们用水、空气中的二氧化碳和阳光制造这种养料。它们通过根从土壤里吸收水分。水通过植物的茎向上运输，并储藏在叶子里。叶子还能收集二氧化碳，然后借助阳光把水和二氧化碳转化成养料。

Food for Energy

To live and grow, meat-eating plants don't just need nutrients from insects.
They also need food for energy.
They make this food using water, a gas from the air called carbon dioxide, and sunlight.
They take in water from the soil through their roots.
The water moves up through the plants' stems and is stored in their leaves.
The leaves also collect carbon dioxide.
Then the leaves use sunlight to turn the water and carbon dioxide into food.

所有的植物都利用水、二氧化碳和阳光生产它们需要的养料，这个过程叫光合作用。

有些食肉植物没有这样的捕虫陷阱，它们通过其他方式捕捉昆虫。试着思考植物可能用哪些方法捕捉昆虫。

- All plants use water, carbon dioxide, and sunlight to make the food they need. This process is called photosynthesis.
- Some meat-eating plants do not have traps. They catch insects in other ways. Try to think of some ways they might do this.

黏糊糊的末端

茅膏菜是一种食肉植物，它们通过散发着香气的黏液诱捕昆虫。它们的叶子被微小的腺毛覆盖，腺毛顶端有一小团黏液。一旦昆虫停在黏黏的腺毛上，就会被困住。叶子快速卷住它的猎物，用黏液覆盖它，昆虫的身体变得又软又烂。然后叶子吸干昆虫的营养物质，直到昆虫只剩下一个躯壳。

茅膏菜的叶子卷住一只苍蝇
a sundew leaf curling around a fly

想象一下，如果你的一位朋友从来没见过茅膏菜，你会怎么描述它呢？

A Sticky End

Sundews are meat-eating plants that use sweet-smelling, sticky glue to trap insects.

Their leaves are covered in tiny stalks that have a blob of glue on the tip.

When an insect lands on a sticky stalk, it gets stuck.

The leaf quickly curls around its victim and covers it with juices that make its body soft and soupy.

Then the leaf soaks up nutrients from the insect until only its shell is left.

Imagine that a friend of yours has never seen a sundew plant. How would you describe it?

茅膏菜的黏液闻起来有股甜味。昆虫停在上面是因为它们以为这是可吸食的花蜜。

茅膏菜分布在图示红色区域。它们生长在潮湿地区柔软的地表。

- The sundew's glue smells sweet. Insects land on it because they think it is nectar that they can feed on.
- Sundews live in the areas shown in red. They grow in wet places with spongy ground.

亮闪闪的捕虫堇

捕虫堇的叶子看起来像被花蜜或者水包裹着一样。然而，当一只昆虫停在它的叶片上，昆虫既吃不到也喝不着，反而会被粘住！捕虫堇的叶子看起来亮闪闪的，因为上面有一层能困住小动物的黏液。它们的叶子还会分泌一种汁液，把昆虫降解成一碗浓汤，然后植物就能吸干它所需要的营养物质。

捕虫堇
butterwort plants

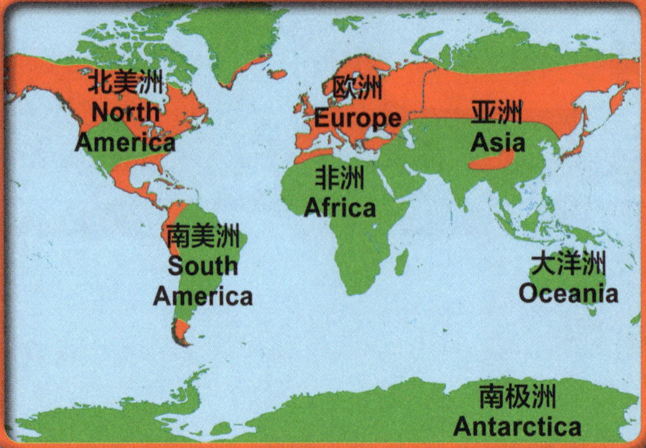

捕虫堇生长于图示红色区域。它们生长在潮湿、柔软的地面。

Shiny Butterworts

A butterwort plant has leaves that look like they are covered in nectar or water. When an insect lands on a leaf, however, it doesn't get a meal or a drink—it gets stuck!

The leaves look shiny because they are covered in sticky glue that traps tiny animals. The leaves also make juices that turn insects into a soupy meal.

Then the plant can soak up the nutrients it needs.

Butterworts live in the areas shown in red. They grow in places with wet, spongy ground.

捕虫堇叶片上的细毛能分泌黏液困住昆虫。不同的细毛能分泌不同的汁液降解动物的身体。

Tiny hairs on a butterwort's leaves make the glue that traps insects. Different hairs make the juices that break up the animal's body.

湿漉漉的顶端

有些食肉植物能把它们捉到的动物淹死。北美洲猪笼草有着长长的笼蔓，也就是捕虫笼，盛有液体。猪笼草的顶部边缘湿滑。如果昆虫沿着边缘爬行，就会滑落淹死。然后，植物会从死去昆虫的身体吸干它所需的营养物质。

北美洲猪笼草
North American pitcher plants

北美洲猪笼草生长在图示红色区域。它们生长地的土壤十分潮湿。

A Watery End

Some meat-eating plants drown the animals they catch.

North American pitcher plants have a long pitcher, or tube, that holds watery liquid.

The top edge of the pitcher plant is slippery.

When an insect walks around the edge, it falls in and drowns.

The plant then soaks up the nutrients it needs from the dead insect's body.

North American pitcher plants live in the areas shown in red. They grow in places where the ground is very wet.

为了防止昆虫逃脱，北美洲猪笼草内部光滑，且有向下生长的绒毛。如果昆虫试图爬出来，就会滑下去掉进液体里。

To stop insects from escaping, the inside of a North American pitcher plant has smooth sections and downward pointing hairs. If an insect tries to climb out, it slides back down into the liquid.

中计被困

加利福尼亚州猪笼草（加州猪笼草）的捕虫笼上方有一个圆形泡泡状的结构。昆虫爬进这个泡泡里吸食植物的花蜜。然而，当它们要出去时，就会感到困惑不已。这些泡泡上有很多透明的斑块，看起来像是可以逃出去的洞。昆虫从一个斑块爬到另一个斑块，试图逃走，直到精疲力竭。最终它们掉进猪笼草的液体里淹死。

加州猪笼草
California pitcher plants

加州猪笼草生长在图示红色区域。它们生长的地区土壤潮湿松软。

Trapped by a Trick

California pitcher plants have a rounded, bubble-like part above their pitchers.
Insects crawl into the bubble to get to the plant's nectar.
When they try to find a way out, however, they get confused.
The bubble has many see-through patches that look like escape holes.
Insects crawl from patch to patch trying to escape until they are worn out.
Then they fall down into the pitcher's liquid and drown.

California pitcher plants live in the areas shown in red. They grow in places where the ground is wet and soft.

加州猪笼草也叫做眼镜蛇百合，因为它们的外形像眼镜蛇。它的叶片看起来像眼镜蛇分叉的舌头。

眼镜蛇
cobra snake

California pitcher plants are also called cobra lilies because they are shaped like a cobra snake. The plants even have leaves that look like a cobra's forked tongue.

当心，昆虫！

食肉植物有许多不同的方法来诱捕动物。有的用黏黏的胶水，有的则淹死它们的猎物。一旦动物被困住，植物就能从昆虫的身体中获取它所需要的营养物质。食肉植物可能看起来很美，闻起来也很香，但如果你是只昆虫，它们就是致命的杀手了！

你最喜欢哪种食肉植物？为什么？

Insects Beware!

Meat-eating plants have many different ways to trap animals.

Some use sticky glue while others drown their meals.

Once an animal is trapped, the plant gets the nutrients it needs from the insect's body.

Meat-eating plants may look pretty and smell sweet, but if you're an insect, they are deadly killers!

Which meat-eating plant did you like the best? Why?

有时，老鼠和小蜥蜴会掉进巨大的猪笼草中被淹死。然后植物会吃掉这些动物以获取它们所需的营养。

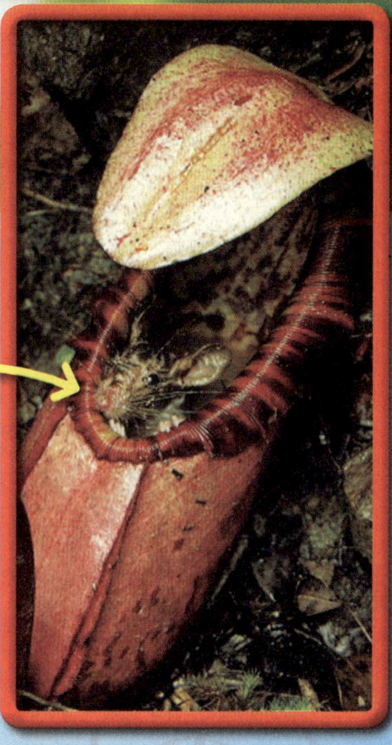

困在猪笼草中的老鼠
a rat stuck in a pitcher plant

Sometimes rats and small lizards fall into large pitcher plants and drown. Then the plants eat these animals to get the nutrients they need.

科学实验室

化身植物学家

有些植物通过捕捉昆虫来获取它们所需的营养。然而，大多数植物都是从土壤中获得营养。将一些豆子种在四种不同类型的土壤中，找出哪种土壤最适合豆子的生长。

土壤1

来自有植物生长的花园或院子的土壤

土壤2

来自没有植物生长的地方的土壤

土壤3

园艺中心的盆栽土

土壤4

沙子或沙质土壤

- 你认为植物在哪种土壤里生长得最好？为什么？
- 在笔记本上写下你的预测。
- 当豆子开始生长时，哪一株生长得最快？哪一株看起来最健康？
- 你觉得为什么你的预测与所发生的情况相符或不相符？

Science Lab

Be a Plant Scientist

Some plants get the nutrients they need by catching insects.

Most plants, however, get nutrients from the soil.

To find out what kind of soil is the best for growing bean seeds, plant some of the seeds in four different types of soil:

Soil 1　Soil from a garden or yard where plants are growing

Soil 2　Soil from an area where plants don't grow

Soil 3　Potting soil from a garden center

Soil 4　Sand or sandy soil

- Which soil do you think the plants will grow best in? Why?
- Write down your prediction in a notebook.
- When the bean plants start to grow, which one grows fastest? Which one looks healthiest?
- Why do you think your prediction did or did not match what happened?

土壤实验的步骤

请一位成年人帮你在网上或园艺中心购买豆子和盆栽土壤。

1. 收集四种类型的土壤。每种土壤都需要足够的量来填满一个小花盆或泡沫塑料杯（底部打孔）。

2. 拿出四个花盆或泡沫塑料杯，将每个花盆或泡沫塑料杯用不同的土壤填满。用记号笔标注每个花盆或杯子。

3. 在每个容器中放入两颗豆子，用土壤覆盖，并轻轻压实。

4. 将花盆或杯子放在阳光充足的窗口。给种子浇水以保持土壤湿润。然后继续观察会发生什么。

Soil experiment step-by-step

Ask a grown-up to help you buy bean seeds and potting soil online or from a garden center.

1. Collect the four types of soil. You will need enough of each soil to fill a small flowerpot or Styrofoam cup (with holes punched in the bottom).
2. Take four pots or Styrofoam cups and fill each one nearly to the top with one type of soil. Use a marker to label each pot or cup.
3. Place two bean seeds in each container, cover them with soil, and press down gently.
4. Place the pots or cups in a sunny window. Water the seeds to keep the soil moist. Then keep watch to see what happens!

附录

科学词汇

能量
energy

气体
gas

昆虫
insect

营养
nutrients

根
roots

腺毛
stalks

吃肉的植物

大部分植物的生长要从土壤里吸收营养，然而，有些植物生长的土壤没有营养。植物是怎么活下去的呢？它们靠吃动物获得营养！本书介绍了吃肉植物用哪些巧妙的方式把小动物们逮个措手不及，引向致命的陷阱。

万物里的科学 不可思议的植物

植物如何净化空气？

植物的传粉

种子是如何传播的？

用阳光烹饪

• 吃肉的植物

天然的药材

责任编辑：周少贞
责任校对：夏洁媛
装帧设计：水长流文化

[英] 埃伦·劳伦斯 著
张潆洁 译

万物里的科学

不可思议的植物

天然的药材

外语教学与研究出版社
FOREIGN LANGUAGE TEACHING AND RESEARCH PRESS

[英] 埃伦•劳伦斯 著
张潆洁 译

万物里的科学

不可思议的植物

天然的药材

外语教学与研究出版社
FOREIGN LANGUAGE TEACHING AND RESEARCH PRESS
北京 BEIJING

京权图字：01-2022-6892

Original English language edition published by Bearport Publishing, Minneapolis, MN, USA.

图书在版编目（CIP）数据

万物里的科学．不可思议的植物．天然的药材 ：汉文、英文 /（英）埃伦·劳伦斯（Ellen Lawrence）著 ；张溸洁译．-- 北京 ：外语教学与研究出版社，2023.6
ISBN 978-7-5213-4508-7

Ⅰ．①万… Ⅱ．①埃… ②张… Ⅲ．①科学知识－儿童读物－汉、英②植物－儿童读物－汉、英 Ⅳ．①Z228.1②Q94-49

中国国家版本馆 CIP 数据核字（2023）第 088253 号

图片来源：
Cover, © anyaivanova/Shutterstock; 3L, © Mrs Ya/Shutterstock; 3TR, © Nattika/Shutterstock; 3BR, © joloei/Shutterstock; 4T, © 2xSamara.com/Shutterstock; 4B, © Fuse/Thinkstock; 5, © gengirl/Shutterstock; 6, © The Print Collector/Alamy; 7, © Erica Olson/FLPA; 8T, © voranat/Shutterstock; 8B, © Swapan Photography/Shutterstock; 9L, © Radka Palenikova/Shutterstock; 9BL, © WILDLIFE GmbH/Alamy; 9BR, © LiliGraphie/Shutterstock; 10T, © lzf/Shutterstock; 10B, © viki2win/Shutterstock; 11, © Vahan Abrahamyan/Shutterstock; 11BR, © Whiteaster/Shutterstock; 12, © Nattika/Shutterstock; 13, © anyaivanova/Shutterstock; 13R, © crystalfoto/Shutterstock; 14, © Wojciech Lisinski/Shutterstock; 15L, © diane555/IstockPhoto; 15, © Jessie Eldora Robertson/Shutterstock; 16T, © azure1/Shutterstock; 16B, © Gita Kulinitch Studio/Shutterstock; 17, © Cowardlion/Shutterstock; 18T, © Amazon-Images MBSI/Alamy; 18B, © H. Zell; 19, © epa European pressphoto agency b.v./Alamy; 20T, © Apiched nakat/Shutterstock; 20B, © joloei/Shutterstock; 21, © Matej Hudovernik/Shutterstock; 21BR, © Rob Hainer/Shutterstock; 22, © ecco/Shutterstock; 23TL, © Image Point Fr/Shutterstock; 23TC, © The Print Collector/Alamy; 23TR, © Africa Studio/Shutterstock; 23BL, © wavebreakmedia/Shutterstock; 23BC, © Africa Studio/Shutterstock; 23BR, © Frank Vassen.

出 版 人　王　芳
项目策划　刘晓楠　贺舒雅
项目负责　贺舒雅
责任编辑　周少贞
责任校对　夏洁媛
装帧设计　水长流文化
出版发行　外语教学与研究出版社
社　　址　北京市西三环北路 19 号（100089）
网　　址　https://www.fltrp.com
印　　刷　天津善印科技有限公司
开　　本　787×1092　1/16
印　　张　9
版　　次　2023 年 6 月第 1 版
　　　　　2023 年 6 月第 1 次印刷
书　　号　ISBN 978-7-5213-4508-7
定　　价　83.00 元（全 6 册）

如有图书采购需求，图书内容或印刷装订等问题，侵权、盗版书籍等线索，请拨打以下电话或关注官方服务号：
客服电话：400 898 7008
官方服务号：微信搜索并关注公众号"外研社官方服务号"
外研社购书网址：https://fltrp.tmall.com

物料号：345080001

记载人类文明
沟通世界文化
www.fltrp.com

目录

来自花园的药材？

阿嚏！哎哟！当人们生病或受伤时，他们可能会去药店。药店出售的药片和药膏是在实验室和工厂里制造的。你知道药品中的一些成分来自植物吗？这些植物生长在草地、森林和花园中。那么，哪些植物可以医治我们呢？让我们一起研究一下！

药房
a pharmacy

Medicine from a Garden?

Achoo! Ouch!

When people are sick or hurt, they might visit a pharmacy.

The pills and ointments sold at these stores are made in labs and factories.

Did you know that some of the ingredients in medicines come from plants?

These plants can be found growing in meadows, forests, and gardens.

So which plants are used to heal us? Let's investigate!

紫锥菊生长在田野和花园里。人们在感冒时服用由紫锥菊制成的药物，感觉会舒服一些。

你认为在有实验室和工厂之前，药品是如何制造的？

Echinacea flowers grow in fields and gardens. People take medicines made from echinacea plants to feel better when they have a cold.

How do you think medicines were made before there were labs and factories?

特殊花园

几百年前，药品并不是在实验室和工厂里制造的。在世界的许多地方，生病的人都会去找药剂师。药剂师使用植物和其他原料配制药品。大多数药剂师都有一个花园，他们在那里种植他们药品配方中的植物。他们将药品做成口服的药水以及药膏出售给人们。

这幅14世纪的画展示了工人在一位药剂师的花园里工作。

药剂师
apothecary

A Special Garden

Hundreds of years ago, medicines weren't made in labs and factories.
In many parts of the world, sick people would visit an apothecary.
An apothecary made medicines using plants and other ingredients.
Most apothecaries had a garden where they grew the plants for their recipes.
They sold their medicines as potions, which people drank, and as ointments.

This painting from the 1400s shows workers in an apothecary's garden.

这个木箱里有蜂巢，蜜蜂在这里制造蜂蜜。

药剂师的治疗方案不仅会用到植物，有时还会用到泥浆、蜂蜜、煮熟的虫子，甚至是人血等原料。

这个现代花园看起来与药剂师的花园类似。

The treatments made by apothecaries didn't only include plants. Sometimes they included ingredients such as mud, honey, boiled worms, and even human blood.

This wooden box contains a beehive where bees make honey.

This modern-day garden looks similar to an apothecary's garden.

制作药品

药剂师在药品中使用根、茎、叶、花和种子。他们用五颜六色的金盏花制作抗菌药品。这种药品被涂在割伤、蜜蜂蜇伤和狗咬伤处。他们还将紫草根煮成糊状，将布浸泡在糊中，然后包扎在断裂的骨头上，使其愈合。

金盏花
calendula flower

药剂师们使用一种叫做研钵和杵的工具来研磨植物。

Making Medicines

Apothecaries used roots, stems, leaves, flowers, and seeds in their medicines.
They made an antiseptic using colorful calendula flowers.
This medicine was put on cuts, bee stings, and dog bites.
They also boiled the roots of comfrey plants to make a paste.
Cloth was soaked in the paste and wrapped around broken bones to heal them.

Apothecaries used a tool called a mortar and pestle to grind up plants.

几百年前，人们身上有跳蚤和虱子是很常见的。药剂师用薰衣草的花制成一种油，人们把油涂抹在身上，用来杀死这些昆虫。

Hundreds of years ago, it was common for people to have fleas and lice. Apothecaries made an oil from lavender flowers that people rubbed on their bodies to kill these insects.

治病的茶

药剂师使用过的许多植物至今仍在沿用，如薄荷。翠绿的薄荷是一种药草。薄荷使一些甜点、牙膏和口香糖具有清凉的口味。薄荷叶也可以用来治疗胃痛。如何使用薄荷治疗胃痛呢？我们将新鲜或干燥的薄荷叶放入热水中，泡成薄荷茶。

薄荷叶
peppermint leaves

薄荷茶
mint tea

一种植物能让食物尝起来辛辣，它被用来治疗关节疼痛，你认为这是哪种植物？

Tea for Healing

Many plants used by apothecaries are still used today, such as peppermint.
The bright green peppermint plant is an herb.
Peppermint gives a minty flavor to some desserts, toothpastes, and chewing gum.
Mint leaves can also be used to treat stomachaches. How?
The fresh or dried leaves are put into hot water and made into a minty tea.

What plant, which makes food taste hot and spicy, do you think is used to heal aching joints?

草地上生长的甘菊花
chamomile flowers growing in a meadow

有睡眠问题的人可以喝甘菊茶来帮助他们入睡。制作这种舒缓的茶需将甘菊花晒干，揉碎，然后泡入热水中。

甘菊干花
dried chamomile flowers

甘菊茶
chamomile tea

People who have trouble sleeping can drink chamomile tea to help them doze off. To make this soothing tea, chamomile flowers are dried, crumbled up, and put into hot water.

舒缓药膏

一些植物可以用来制作舒缓药膏。辣椒含有一种化学物质，使其尝起来很辛辣。这种化学物质可用于制作软膏，涂抹在膝盖等疼痛的关节上。另一种有治疗作用的植物是芦荟。它尖尖的叶子里的凝胶状叶肉具有冷却和舒缓的作用。将凝胶涂抹在皮肤上，可以治疗晒伤和蜇伤。

辣椒
chili peppers

Soothing Ointments

Some plants can be used to make soothing ointments.

Chili peppers contain a chemical that makes them taste spicy and feel hot.

This chemical is used in ointments that are rubbed on aching joints such as knees.

Another healing plant is aloe vera.

The gel-like flesh inside its pointy leaves is cooling and soothing.

The gel is rubbed onto the skin to treat sunburns and stings.

芦荟
aloe vera plant

芦荟胶不仅对人类有治疗作用，对动物也有。兽医和宠物的主人用这种凝胶来治疗动物皮肤上的疮疡。

芦荟内的凝胶
gel inside an aloe plant

Aloe vera gel is not only healing for humans but for animals, too. Vets and pet owners can use the gel to treat sores on an animal's skin.

来自树木的药材

不仅小型植物可以治病，高大的树木也可以。美洲原住民曾经收集柳树的树皮，他们将树皮切碎，混入热水，制成饮料。这种饮料被用作退烧药，还可用作止痛药治疗头痛和牙痛。时至今日，柳树皮仍被用来制作止痛药。

柳树的树皮
bark on the trunk of a willow tree

Medicine from Trees

It's not only small plants that can heal—trees can, too.
Native Americans once collected bark from willow trees.
They shredded the bark and mixed it with hot water to make a drink.
This drink was used as a fever reducer and as a painkiller to treat headaches and toothaches.
Willow bark is still used today to make pain medicines.

柳树皮含有一种叫水杨酸的化学物质。19世纪末，科学家发明了如何利用水杨酸制造阿司匹林。今天，世界各地的人们都把阿司匹林用作止痛药，并用来辅助治疗心脏问题。

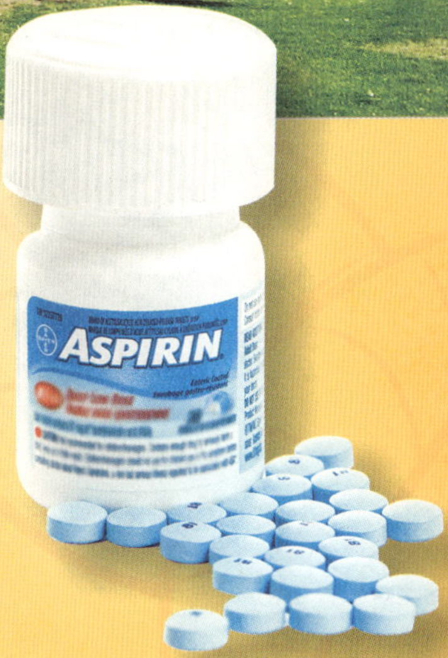

Willow bark contains a chemical called salicin. In the late 1800s, scientists discovered how to use salicin to make aspirin. Today, people around the world take aspirin as a painkiller and to help treat heart problems.

银杏树

还有一种树，在世界各地的许多城市都有，可以帮助人们治病。银杏树的叶片含有一种化学物质，有助于改善大脑功能。银杏叶被晒干后混入药片，人们服用这些药片来帮助他们增强记忆力。

哪里是寻找新型药用植物的好地方？

Ginkgo Trees

There's another tree, found in many cities around the world, that can help heal people.

The leaves of ginkgo trees contain a chemical that helps improve brain function.

The leaves are dried and made into pills.

People take these pills to help strengthen their memories.

- Where would be a good place to look for new types of healing plants?

日本某城市的银杏树
ginkgo trees in a city in Japan

银杏还可用于帮助阿尔茨海默病的患者。这种疾病通常影响老年人，导致他们失去记忆。

Ginkgo is also used to help people with a disease called Alzheimer's. This disease usually affects older people and causes them to lose their memories.

来自雨林的药材

雨林是超过17万种不同种类植物的家园！数百年来，生活在南美洲雨林中的人们一直都在用植物治病。他们用猫爪藤治疗疼痛和皮肤感染，用金钮扣的汁液来治疗牙痛。

猫爪藤
cat's claw plant

金钮扣的花朵
jambu flower

Rain Forest Medicines

Rain forests are home to more than 170,000 different types of plants!
People who live in South American rain forests have been healing with plants for hundreds of years.
They use the cat's claw plant to treat pain and skin infections.
Juices from the jambu plant are used to cure toothaches.

印度尼西亚明打威部落的一名男子在雨林中寻找治病的植物。

科学家们认为，雨林中可能还有数千种新植物有待发现。这些植物中可能含有可以治疗和治愈疾病的化学物质。

- Scientists believe there could be thousands of new plants still to be discovered in rain forests. Many of these plants may contain chemicals that could treat and cure illnesses.
- A man from the Mentawai tribe in Indonesia searches for healing plants in a rain forest.

拯救生命的花朵

一种来自非洲马达加斯加岛的雨林植物甚至被用来治疗癌症。多年来，许多儿童死于一种叫做白血病的癌症。20世纪50年代，科学家发现长春花含有一种抗癌的化学物质。现在，用这种植物制成的药品每年都能拯救成千上万儿童的生命！

马达加斯加长春花
Madagascar periwinkle

A Flower That Saves Lives

One rain forest plant from the African island of Madagascar has even been used to treat cancer.

For years, many children died from a type of cancer called leukemia.

In the 1950s, scientists discovered that the Madagascar periwinkle contains a cancer-fighting chemical.

Now, medicines made with this plant save the lives of thousands of children each year!

印度尼西亚雨林中的红毛猩猩
an orangutan in a rain forest in Indonesia

不仅人类将热带雨林植物用作药物，红毛猩猩也吃一种特殊植物的花来治疗头疼。它们还咀嚼鸭跖草的叶片，把吐出的混合物涂抹在身上，以治疗疼痛。

鸭跖草
commelina plant

It's not only humans that use rain forest plants as medicines. Orangutans eat serantung flowers to treat headaches. They also chew up commelina leaves and rub the spitty mixture onto their bodies to heal aches and pains.

科学实验室

一本关于治病植物的书

做一本你自己的书，教朋友和家人有关治病植物的知识吧。书中要包含本书中你认为最有趣的植物。你也可以利用互联网来了解其他可以治病的植物。

Science Lab

A Healing Plants Book

Make your own book to teach friends and family members about healing plants.
Include the plants from this book that you think are the most interesting.
You can also use the Internet to learn about other healing plants.

如何制作自己的书

1. 请一位成年人将两张纸订在一起。
2. 在每页纸的顶部写上一种治病植物的名字。
3. 研究每种植物的相关知识。
4. 然后就每种植物写两三句话，并画图来说明这些知识。
5. 与朋友和家人分享你的书。

在研究治病植物时，请思考以下问题。把答案包含在你提供的信息中。

- 植物的哪一部分用来制作药品？
- 植物是如何帮助人们治病的？

How to Make Your Book

1. Have an adult staple two pieces of paper together.
2. Write the name of a healing plant at the top of each page.
3. Research facts about each plant.
4. Then write two or three sentences about each one and draw pictures to illustrate the facts.
5. Share your book with friends and family members.

Think about these questions when you are researching healing plants. Include the answers in your information.

- Which part of the plant is used to make a medicine?
- How does this plant help heal people?

附录

科学词汇

抗菌剂
antiseptic

药剂师
apothecary

药草
herb

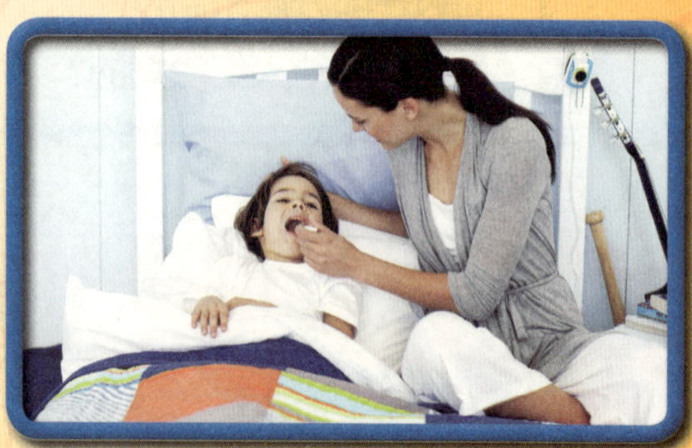

感染
infections

药膏
ointments

雨林
rain forests

天然的药材

有些植物可以帮助愈合伤口和治疗疾病，有些植物可以用来舒缓晒伤，柳树的树皮可以用作止痛剂，雨林中的花朵可以帮助治疗癌症。来自世界各地的植物能够治愈各种不同的疾病。让我们一起来了解一下这些天然的药材吧！

万物里的科学

不可思议的植物

植物如何净化空气？　　用阳光烹饪

植物的传粉　　吃肉的植物

种子是如何传播的？　　• 天然的药材

责任编辑：周少贞
责任校对：夏洁媛
装帧设计：水长流文化